GROWING UP DAKOTA

by
Charles Alexander Eastman

Edited and Illustrated
by Charlene Notgrass

Cover image was inspired by
Dog Travois/Blackfoot Camp
by Edwin Willard Deming (1860-1942)
Smithsonian American Art Museum,
Bequest of Victor Justice Evans

ISBN 978-1-60999-162-3

Indian Boyhood originally published by McClure, Phillips, and Company in 1902. *Indian Child Life* originally published in 1913 by Little, Brown, and Company.

This edition © 2020 by Notgrass History

Cover design and illustration and all interior illustrations
by Charlene Notgrass
Interior design by Charlene Notgrass

Printed and Bound in the United States of America

NOTGRASS
HISTORY
Gainesboro, Tennessee
notgrass.com

WHY I WRITE ABOUT NATIVE NATIONS

I was born in 1953 in a small town in Tennessee. My only contact with Native Americans when I was a child was when our family visited the Great Smoky Mountains. We did this several times during my childhood. On some trips, we drove across the mountains from Gatlinburg, Tennessee, to Cherokee, North Carolina, which is home to many Overhill Cherokees. One time we went to Cherokee with my parents, brother, grandparents, and young aunt, just a year and a half older than I. We saw a Cherokee man dressed up in a warbonnet. He was offering to pose for pictures. Someone in our family paid for him to have his picture made with my aunt and me. On one trip I brought home a small beaded doll as a souvenir, and another time I brought home a beaded headband.

By 1986 I was all grown-up with a husband and three young children. We went on a family camping vacation to see Mount Rushmore in the Black Hills of South Dakota. One evening a few members of a native nation came to our campground to dance native dances with us. Though I don't know for sure, they were likely members of a Dakota nation. Our two-year-old daughter was standing beside one of the young men when we all took hands to form a circle. We have a wonderful photograph of her looking up at him. I remember feeling that I should say, "I am sorry for all of the ways that white people have mistreated your people."

When I began to write about history for children, I made a conscious decision to honor native nations in my writing. I am happy to share with you some of Charles Alexander Eastman's memories of his childhood.

Eastman was born in 1858 in a native village in Minnesota. His father, Ite Wakanhdi Ota (which means Many Lightnings), was a full-blooded Dakota. His mother, Wakan Tanka Win, was half-Dakota. Her mother was a full-blooded Dakota. Her father was a U.S. Army officer.

Wakan Tanka Win died when Eastman was an infant. He was given the name Hakadah which means "The Pitiful Last." His grandmother lovingly cared for him after his mother's death. A war between the United States Army and the Dakota people separated Hakadah from his father when Hakadah was about four years old. While Hakadah was a boy, his name was changed to

Ohiyesa, which means "winner."

When Ohiyesa was fifteen years old, his father got a native guide to help him search for Ohiyesa. After they found him, his father brought him to live on his homestead in South Dakota. He told Ohiyesa that they were going to live like the white men. He told him to choose a new name. His father had chosen Jacob Eastman for his own name. Ohiyesa chose Charles Alexander Eastman. Charles started to school and liked it. He continued his education until he graduated from Dartmouth College and Boston University's medical school. He became a physician.

Charles Eastman had respect for native ways and for white ways. Eastman wrote eleven books. I have chosen excerpts from his books *Indian Child Life* (1913) and *Indian Boyhood* (1902) to create *Growing Up Dakota*.

Many of Eastman's stories are about his own life, but he also tells stories about his grandmother and a girl named Winona. Both boys and girls will enjoy *Growing Up Dakota*.

Eastman lived from 1858 to 1939. He wrote in ways that communicated well to the readers of his time. He used words that are offensive to us today, words such as pale-face, savage, half-breed, red man, and primitive. However, Eastman loved and respected his people. He meant what he wrote to be respectful of them. The words that people find acceptable change over time.

Eastman lived through the American Civil War. He wrote about the terrible shame of slavery.

All of the words in *Growing Up Dakota* are the original words of Charles Eastman, except when you see lines and type like this:

The italicized words between the lines are mine.

I have also left Eastman's spelling and punctuation.

The Dakota people had a longstanding conflict with the Ojibwe nation (Eastman spelled it Ojibway) and also with white people. You will read about those conflicts in this book. These are sad stories, but they are a real part of history. Eastman refers to his people as Sioux. Today many members of Eastman's native nation prefer to call themselves Dakota.

I have not changed the words that Eastman chose because I want you to be able to read this story in the words of the real Dakota man who wrote them. I did, however, change some of the chapter titles.

With great respect for the Dakota, the Ojibwe, and white Americans, I offer to you *Growing Up Dakota* — in Charles Alexander Eastman's own words. He meant no disrespect and neither do I. He wanted people to understand. So do I.

It is quite a story. Enjoy.

Charlene Notgrass, 2020

A LETTER TO CHILDREN
from Charles Alexander Eastman, 1915

Dear Children:—You will like to know that the man who wrote these true stories is himself one of the people he describes so pleasantly and so lovingly for you. He hopes that when you have finished this book, the Indians will seem to you very real and very friendly. He is not willing that all your knowledge of the race that formerly possessed this continent should come from the lips of strangers and enemies, or that you should think of them as blood-thirsty and treacherous, as savage and unclean.

War, you know, is always cruel, and it is true that there were stern fighting men among the Indians, as well as among your own forefathers. But there were also men of peace, men generous and kindly and religious. There were tender mothers, and happy little ones, and a home life that was pure and true. There were high ideals of loyalty and honor. It will do you good and make you happier to read of these things.

Perhaps you wonder how a "real, live Indian" could write a book. I will tell you how. The story of this man's life is itself as wonderful as a fairy tale. Born in a wigwam, as he has told you, and early left motherless, he was brought up, like the little Hiawatha, by a good grandmother. When he was four years old, war broke out between his people and the United States government. The Indians were defeated and many of them were killed. Some fled northward into Canada and took refuge under the British flag, among them the writer of this book, with his grandmother and an uncle. His father was captured by the whites.

In 1855 Henry Wadsworth Longfellow wrote "The Song of Hiawatha," based on a traditional Native American oral history.

After ten years of that wild life, now everywhere at an end, of which he has given you a true picture in his books, his father, whom the good President Lincoln had pardoned and released from the military prison, made the long and dangerous journey to Canada to find and bring back his youngest son. The Sioux were beginning to learn that the old life must go, and that, if they were to survive at all, they must follow "the white man's road," long and hard as it looked to a free people. They were beginning to plow and sow and send their children to school.

Ohiyesa, the Winner, as the boy was called, came home with his father to what was then Dakota Territory, to a little settlement of Sioux homesteaders. Everything about the new life was strange to him, and at first he did not like it at all. He had thoughts of running away and making his way back to Canada. But his father, Many Lightnings, who had been baptized a Christian under the name of Jacob Eastman, told him that he, too, must take a new name, and he chose that of Charles Alexander Eastman. He was told to cut off his long hair and put on citizen's clothing. Then his father made him choose between going to school and working at the plow.

Ohiyesa tried plowing for half a day. It was hard work to break the tough prairie sod with his father's oxen and the strange implement they gave him. He decided to try school. Rather to his surprise, he liked it, and he kept on. His teachers were pleased with his progress, and soon better opportunities opened to him. He was sent farther east to a better school, where he continued to do well, and soon went higher. In the long summer vacations he worked, on farms, in shops and offices; and in winter he studied and played football and all the other games you play, until after about fifteen or sixteen years he found himself with the diplomas of a famous college and a great university, a Bachelor of Science, a Doctor of Medicine, and a doubly educated man—educated in the lore of the wilderness as well as in some of the deepest secrets of civilization.

Since that day, a good many more years have passed. Ohiyesa, known as Doctor Charles A. Eastman, has now a home and six children of his own among the New England hills. He has hundreds of devoted friends of both races. He is the author of five books which have been widely read, some of them in England, France and Germany as well as in America, and he speaks face to face to thousands of people every year. Perhaps some of you have heard from his own lips his recollections of wild life. You may find all the stories in this book, and many more of the same sort, in the books called "Indian Boyhood," and "Old Indian Days," published by Doubleday, Page and Company, of Garden City, L.I., who have kindly consented to the publication of this little volume in order that the children in our schools might read stories of real Indians by a real Indian.

CONTENTS

From *Indian Child Life*

1 "The Pitiful Last" 1
2 Moving to a Safe Place 7
3 Sugar Camp 15
4 Games and Sports 20
5 An Indian Boy's Training 27
6 The Boy Hunter 35
7 Evening in the Lodge 40
8 When Winona Was a Little Girl 49
9 Winona Becomes a Young Maiden 54
10 Midsummer Feast and Ballgame 61

From *Indian Boyhood*

11 Earliest Memories 68
12 Uncheedah, My Grandmother 74
13 Mothers, Fathers, and Children 82

14	Playmates	84
15	Smoky Day, the Storyteller	92
16	The Maidens' Feast	97
17	The Fall Hunt	102
18	Winter Camp	110
19	Happy Harvest Days	119
20	A Meeting on the Plains	121
21	The Funny Philosopher	125
22	First Impressions of the White Man's World	131

1

"THE PITIFUL LAST"

What boy would not be an Indian for a while when he thinks of the freest life in the world? This life was mine. Every day there was a real hunt. There was real game.

No people have a better use of their five senses than the children of the wilderness. We could smell as well as hear and see. We could feel and taste as well as we could see and hear. Nowhere has the memory been more fully developed than in the wild life, and I can still see wherein I owe much to my early training.

Of course I myself do not remember when I first saw the day, but my brothers have often recalled the event with much mirth; for it was a custom of the Sioux that when a boy was born his brother must plunge into the water, or roll in the snow naked if it was winter time; and if he was not big enough to do either of these himself, water was thrown on him. If the new-born had a sister, she must be immersed. The idea was that a warrior had come to camp, and the other children must display some act of hardihood.

I was so unfortunate as to be the youngest of five children who, soon after I was born, were left motherless. I had to bear the humiliating name "Hakādah," meaning "the pitiful last," until I should earn a more dignified and appropriate name. I was regarded as little more than a plaything by the rest of the children.

The babe was done up as usual in a movable cradle made from an oak board two and a half feet long and one and a half feet wide. On one side of it was nailed with brass-headed tacks the richly embroidered sack, which was open in front and laced up and down with buckskin strings. Over the arms of the infant was a wooden bow, the ends of which were firmly attached to the board, so that if the cradle should fall the child's head and face would be protected.

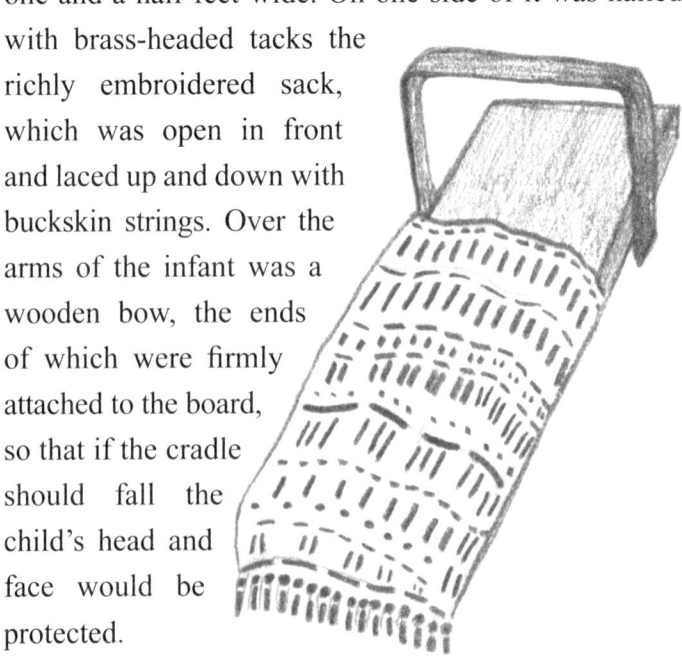

On this bow were hung curious playthings—strings of artistically carved bones and hoofs of deer, which rattled when the little hands moved them.

In this upright cradle I lived, played, and slept the greater part of the time during the first few months of my life. Whether I was made to lean against a lodge pole or was suspended from a bough of a tree, while my grandmother cut wood, or whether I was carried on her back, or conveniently balanced by another child in a similar cradle hung on the opposite side of a pony, I was still in my oaken bed.

Hakadah's ancestors did not use ponies or horses until after Spanish people brought horses to North America.

This grandmother, who had already lived through sixty years of hardships, was a wonder to the young maidens of the tribe. She showed no less enthusiasm over Hakadah than she had done when she held her first-born, the boy's father, in her arms. Every little attention that is due to a loved child she performed with much skill and devotion. She made all my scanty garments and my tiny moccasins with a great deal of taste. It was said by all that I could not have had more attention had my mother been living.

Uncheedah (grandmother) was a great singer. Sometimes, when Hakadah wakened too early in the morning, she would sing to him something like the following lullaby:

Sleep, sleep, my boy, the Chippewas
Are far away—are far away.
Sleep, sleep, my boy; prepare to meet
The foe by day—the foe by day!
The cowards will not dare to fight
Till morning break—till morning break.
Sleep, sleep, my child, while still 'tis night;
Then bravely wake—then bravely wake!

The Dakota women were wont to cut and bring their fuel from the woods and, in fact, to perform most of the drudgery of the camp. This of necessity fell to their lot because the men must follow the game during the day. Very often my grandmother carried me with her on these excursions; and while she worked it was her habit to suspend me from a wild grape vine or a springy bough, so that the least breeze would swing the cradle to and fro.

She has told me that when I had grown old enough to take notice, I was apparently capable of holding extended conversations in an unknown dialect with birds and red squirrels. Once I fell asleep in my cradle, suspended five or six feet from the ground, while Uncheedah was some distance away, gathering birch bark for a canoe. A squirrel had found it convenient to come upon the bow of my cradle and nibble his hickory nut, until he awoke me by dropping the crumbs of his meal. It was a common thing for birds to alight on my cradle in the woods.

After I left my cradle, I almost walked away from it, she told me. She then began calling my attention to natural objects. Whenever I heard the song of a bird, she would tell me what bird it came from, something after this fashion:

"Hakadah, listen to Shechoka (the robin) calling his mate. He says he has just found something good to eat." Or "Listen to Oopehanska (the thrush); he is singing for his little wife. He will sing his best." When in the evening the whippoorwill started his song with vim, no further than a stone's throw from our tent in the woods, she would say to me:

"Hush! It may be an Ojibway scout!"

Again, when I waked at midnight, she would say:

"Do not cry! Hinakaga (the owl) is watching you from the tree-top."

Hakadah usually covered his head when he heard an owl hoot. Native scouts who were on the war-path often imitated owls, so adults taught children to be wary when they heard them.

Indian children were trained so that they hardly ever cried much in the night. This was very expedient and necessary in their exposed life. In my infancy it was my grandmother's custom to put me to sleep, as she said, with the birds, and to waken me with them, until it became a habit. She did this with an object in view. An Indian must always rise early. In the first place, as a hunter, he finds his game best at daybreak. Secondly, other tribes, when on the war-path, usually make their attack very early in the morning. Even when our people are moving about leisurely, we like to rise before daybreak, in order to travel when the air is cool, and unobserved, perchance, by our enemies.

As a little child, it was instilled into me to be silent and reticent. This was one of the most important traits to form in the character of the Indian. As a hunter and warrior it was considered absolutely necessary to him, and was thought to lay the foundations of patience and self-control.

2

MOVING TO A SAFE PLACE

One of the earliest recollections of my adventurous childhood is the ride I had on a pony's side. I was passive in the whole matter. A little girl cousin of mine was put in a bag and suspended from the horn of an Indian saddle; but her weight must be balanced or the saddle would not remain on the animal's back. Accordingly, I was put into another sack and made to keep the saddle and the girl in position! I did not object, for I had a very pleasant game of peek-a-boo with the little girl, until we came to a big snow-drift, where the poor beast was stuck fast and began to lie down. Then it was not so nice!

This was the convenient and primitive way in which some mothers packed their children for winter journeys. However cold the weather might be, the inmate of the fur-lined sack was usually very comfortable—at least I used to think so. I believe I was accustomed to all the precarious Indian conveyances, and, as a boy, I enjoyed the dog-travaux ride as much as any. The travaux consisted of a set of rawhide strips securely lashed to the tent-poles, which were harnessed to the sides of the animal as if he stood between shafts, while the free ends were allowed to drag on the ground. Both ponies and large dogs were used as beasts of burden, and they carried in this way the smaller children as well as the baggage.

This mode of travelling for children was possible only in the summer, and as the dogs were sometimes unreliable, the little ones were exposed to a certain amount of danger. For instance, whenever a train of dogs had been travelling for a long time, almost perishing with the heat and their heavy loads, a glimpse of water would cause them to forget all their responsibilities. Some of them, in spite of the screams of the women, would swim with their burdens into the cooling stream, and I was thus, on more than one occasion, made to partake of an unwilling bath.

When Hakadah was four years old, American soldiers and Dakota Sioux fought in the U.S.-Dakota War of 1862. Hakadah and his family fled from Minnesota.

In the general turmoil, we took flight into British Columbia, and the journey is still vividly remembered by all our family. A yoke of oxen and a lumber-wagon were taken from some white farmer and brought home for our conveyance.

How delighted I was when I learned that we were to ride behind those wise-looking animals and in that gorgeously painted wagon! It seemed almost like a living creature to me, this new vehicle with four legs, and the more so when we got out of axle-grease and the wheels went along squealing like pigs!

The boys found a great deal of innocent fun in jumping from the high wagon while the oxen were leisurely moving along. My elder brothers soon became experts. At last, I mustered up courage enough to join them in this sport. I was sure they stepped on the wheel, so I cautiously placed my moccasined foot upon it.

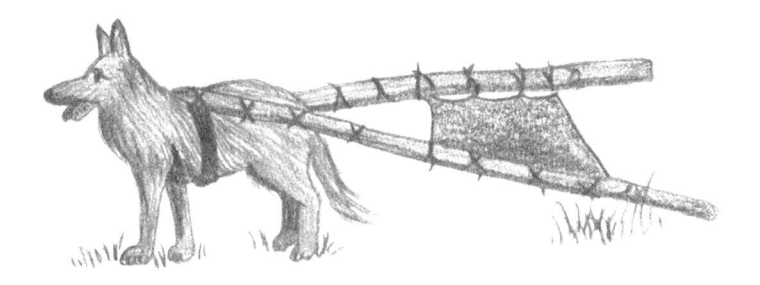

Alas, before I could realize what had happened, I was under the wheels, and had it not been for the neighbor immediately behind us, I might have been run over by the next team as well

This was my first experience with a civilized vehicle. I cried out all possible reproaches on the white man's team and concluded that a dog-travaux was good enough for me. I was really rejoiced that we were moving away from the people who made the wagon that had almost ended my life, and it did not occur to me that I alone was to blame. I could not be persuaded to ride in that wagon again and was glad when we finally left it beside the Missouri river.

The next summer American General Henry Sibley pursued Hakadah's people across the Missouri River.

Now the Missouri is considered one of the most treacherous rivers in the world. Even a good modern boat is not safe upon its uncertain current. We were forced to cross in buffalo-skin boats—as round as tubs!

The Washechu (white men) were coming in great numbers with their big guns, and while most of our men were fighting them to gain time, the women and the old men made and equipped the temporary boats, braced with ribs of willow. Some of these were towed by two or three women or men swimming in the water and some by ponies. It was not an easy matter to keep them right side up, with their helpless freight of little children and such goods as we possessed.

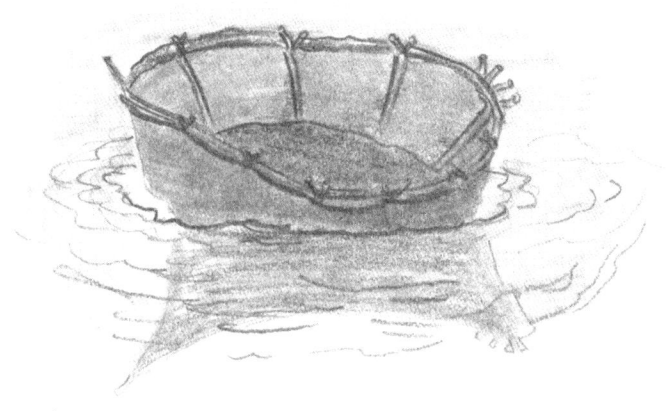

In our flight, we little folks were strapped in the saddles or held in front of an older person, and in the long night marches to get away from the soldiers, we suffered from loss of sleep and insufficient food. Our meals were eaten hastily, and sometimes in the saddle. Water was not always to be found. The people carried it with them in bags formed of tripe or the dried pericardium of animals.

Now we were compelled to trespass upon the country of hostile tribes and were harassed by them almost daily and nightly. Only the strictest vigilance saved us.

One day we met with another enemy near the British lines. It was a prairie fire. We were surrounded. Another fire was quickly made, which saved our lives.

One of the most thrilling experiences of the following winter was a blizzard, which overtook us in our wanderings. Here and there, a family lay down in the snow, selecting a place where it was not likely to drift much. For a day and a night we lay under the snow. Uncle stuck a long pole beside us to tell us when the storm was over. We had plenty of buffalo robes and the snow kept us warm, but we found it heavy. After a time, it became packed and hollowed out around our bodies, so that we were as comfortable as one can be under those circumstances.

The next day the storm ceased, and we discovered a large herd of buffaloes almost upon us. We dug our way out, shot some of the buffaloes, made a fire and enjoyed a good dinner.

I was now an exile as well as motherless; yet I was not unhappy. Our wanderings from place to place afforded us many pleasant experiences and quite as many hardships and misfortunes. There were times of plenty and times of scarcity, and we had several narrow escapes from death. In savage life, the early spring is the most trying time and almost all the famines occurred at this period of the year.

The Indians are a patient and a clannish people; their love for one another is stronger than that of any civilized people I know.

Children were not able to handle hunger as well as the old people. When food was scarce, the adults often went without food themselves to make it last as long as possible for the children.

I once passed through one of these hard springs when we had nothing to eat for several days. I well remember the six small birds which constituted the breakfast for six families one morning; and then we had no dinner or supper to follow! What a relief that was to me—although I had only a small wing of a small bird for my share! Soon after this, we came into a region where buffaloes were plenty, and hunger and scarcity were forgotten.

Such was the Indians' wild life! When game was to be had and the sun shone, they easily forgot the bitter experiences of the winter before. Little preparation was made for the future.

In summer . . .

. . . it seems to me that no life is happier than his! Food is free—lodging free—everything free! All were alike rich in the summer, and, again, all were alike poor in the winter and early spring. However, their diseases were fewer and not so destructive as now, and the Indian's health was generally good. The Indian boy enjoyed such a life as almost all boys dream of and would choose for themselves if they were permitted to do so.

The raids made upon our people by other tribes were frequent, and we had to be constantly on the watch. I remember at one time a night attack was made upon our camp and all our ponies stampeded. Only a few of them were recovered, and our journeys after this misfortune were effected mostly by means of the dog-travaux.

A man who was half-native and half-white betrayed Hakadah's father and two older brothers to United States authorities.

As I was then living with my uncle in another part of the country, I became separated from them for ten years. During all this time we believed that they had been killed by the whites, and I was taught that I must avenge their deaths as soon as I was able to go upon the war-path.

3

SUGAR CAMP

With the first March thaw the thoughts of the Indian women of my childhood days turned promptly to the annual sugar-making. This industry was chiefly followed by the old men and women and the children. The rest of the tribe went out upon the spring fur-hunt at this season, leaving us at home to make the sugar.

The first and most important of the necessary utensils were the huge iron and brass kettles for boiling. Everything else could be made, but these must be bought, begged or borrowed.

The Dakota and other native nations purchased iron, brass, and tin objects from Americans or Canadians.

A maple tree was felled and a log canoe hollowed out, into which the sap was to be gathered. Little troughs of basswood and birchen basins were also made to receive the sweet drops as they trickled from the tree.

As soon as these labors were accomplished, we all proceeded to the bark sugar house, which stood in the midst of a fine grove of maples on the bank of the Minnesota river. We found this hut partially filled with the snows of winter and the withered leaves of the preceding autumn, and it must be cleared for our use. In the meantime a tent was pitched outside for a few days' occupancy. The snow was still deep in the woods, with a solid crust upon which we could easily walk; for we usually moved to the sugar house before the sap had actually started, the better to complete our preparations.

My grandmother did not confine herself to canoe-making. She also collected a good supply of fuel for the fires, for she would not have much time to gather wood when the sap began to flow. Presently the weather moderated and the snow began to melt. The month of April brought showers which carried most of it off into the Minnesota river. Now the women began to test the trees—moving leisurely among them, axe in hand, and striking a single quick blow, to see if the sap would appear.

Some trees were ready for the sap to flow and others were not.

Now one of the birchen basins was set under each tree, and a hardwood chip driven deep into the cut which the axe had made. From the corners of this chip—at first drop by drop, then, more freely—the sap trickled into the little dishes.

It is usual to make sugar from maples, but several other trees were also tapped by the Indians. From the birch and ash was made a dark-colored sugar, with a somewhat bitter taste, which was used for medicinal purposes. The box-elder yielded a beautiful white sugar, whose only fault was that there was never enough of it!

A long fire was now made in the sugar house, and a row of brass kettles suspended over the blaze. The sap was collected by the women in tin or birchen buckets and poured into the canoes, from which the kettles were kept filled. The hearts of the boys beat high with pleasant anticipations when they heard the welcome hissing sound of the boiling sap! Each boy claimed one kettle for his especial charge. It was his duty to see that the fire was kept under it, to watch lest it boil over, and finally, when the sap became sirup, to test it upon the snow, dipping it out with a wooden paddle. So frequent were these tests that for the first day or two we consumed nearly all that could be made; and it was not until the sweetness began to pall that my grandmother set herself in earnest to store up sugar for future use. She made it into cakes of various forms, in birchen molds, and sometimes in hollow canes or reeds, and the bills of ducks and geese. Some of it was pulverized and packed in rawhide cases.

Being a prudent woman, she did not give it to us after the first month or so, except upon special occasions, and it was thus made to last almost the year around. The smaller candies were reserved as an occasional treat for the little fellows, and the sugar was eaten at feasts with wild rice or parched corn, and also with pounded dried meat. Coffee and tea, with their substitutes, were all unknown to us in those days.

Every pursuit has its trials and anxieties. My grandmother's special tribulations, during the sugaring season, were the upsetting and gnawing of holes in her birch-bark pans. The transgressors were the rabbit and squirrel tribes, and we little boys for once became useful, in shooting them with our bows and arrows. We hunted all over the sugar camp, until the little creatures were fairly driven out of the neighborhood. Occasionally one of my older brothers brought home a rabbit or two, and then we had a feast.

I remember on this occasion of our last sugar bush in Minnesota, that I stood one day outside of our hut and watched the approach of a visitor—a bent old man, his hair almost white, and carrying on his back a large bundle of red willow, or kinnikinick, which the Indians use for smoking. He threw down his load at the door and thus saluted us: "You have indeed perfect weather for sugar-making."

It was my great-grandfather, Cloud Man, whose original village was on the shores of Lakes Calhoun and Harriet, now in the suburbs of the city of Minneapolis. He was the first Sioux chief to welcome the Protestant missionaries among his people, and a well-known character in those pioneer days.

Cloud Man brought word that a band of Ojibwe had attacked peaceful sugarmakers. Hakadah and his people were concerned but they were able to return safely to their village with much sugar for the winter.

4

GAMES AND SPORTS

The Indian boy was a prince of the wilderness. He had but very little work to do during the period of his boyhood. His principal occupation was the practice of a few simple arts in warfare and the chase. Aside from this, he was master of his time.

It is true that our savage life was a precarious one, and full of dreadful catastrophes; however, this never prevented us from enjoying our sports to the fullest extent.

The life of an Indian boy had many dangers, but Hakadah and his friends accepted this.

Our sports were molded by the life and customs of our people; indeed, we practiced only what we expected to do when grown. Our games were feats with the bow and arrow, foot and pony races, wrestling, swimming and imitation of the customs and habits of our fathers. We had sham fights with mud balls and willow wands; we played lacrosse, made war upon bees, shot winter arrows (which were used only in that season), and coasted upon the ribs of animals and buffalo robes.

No sooner did the boys get together than, as a usual thing, they divided into squads and chose sides; then a leading arrow was shot at random into the air. Before it fell to the ground a volley from the bows of the participants followed. Each player was quick to note the direction and speed of the leading arrow and he tried to send his own at the same speed and at an equal height, so that when it fell it would be closer to the first than any of the others.

It was considered out of place to shoot by first sighting the object aimed at. This was usually impracticable in actual life, because the object was almost always in motion, while the hunter himself was often upon the back of a pony at full gallop. Therefore, it was the off-hand shot that the Indian boy sought to master.

Boys had races almost every day. At noon they gathered near a body of water. They watered their ponies and let them graze for an hour or two.

A boy might say to some other whom he considered his equal: "I can't run; but I will challenge you to fifty paces."

A former hero, when beaten, would often explain his defeat by saying: "I drank too much water."

Boys of all ages were paired for a "spin," and the little red men cheered on their favorites with spirit.

As soon as this was ended, the pony races followed. All the speedy ponies were picked out and riders chosen. If a boy declined to ride, there would be shouts of derision.

Last of all came the swimming. A little urchin would hang to his pony's long tail, while the latter, with only his head above water, glided sportively along. Finally the animals were driven into a fine field of grass and we turned our attention to other games.

The "mud-and-willow" fight was rather a severe and dangerous sport. A lump of soft clay was stuck on the end of a limber and springy willow wand and thrown as boys throw apples from sticks, with considerable force. When there were fifty or a hundred players on each side, the battle became warm; but anything to arouse the bravery of Indian boys seemed to them a good and wholesome diversion.

Wrestling was largely indulged in by us all. It may seem odd, but wrestling was done by a great many boys at once—from ten to any number on a side. It was really a battle, in which each one chose his opponent. The rule was that if a boy sat down, he was let alone, but as long as he remained standing within the field, he was open to an attack. No one struck with the hand, but all manner of tripping with legs and feet and butting with the knees was allowed. Altogether it was an exhausting pastime— fully equal to the American game of football, and only the young athlete could really enjoy it.

One of our most curious sports was a war upon the nests of wild bees. We imagined ourselves about to make an attack upon the Ojibways or some tribal foe. We all painted and stole cautiously upon the nest; then, with a rush and war-whoop, sprang upon the object of our attack and endeavored to destroy it. But it seemed that the bees were always on the alert and never entirely surprised, for they always raised quite as many scalps as did their bold assailants!

The boys did a native dance when they finished attacking a bee nest. I hope none of them were allergic to bee stings!

On the occasion of my first experience in this mode of warfare, there were two other little boys who were also novices. One of them particularly was really too young to indulge in an exploit of that kind.

When Hakadah and his friends finished an attack on the bees, they announced their success with a loud voice.

My friend, Little Wound (as I will call him, for I do not remember his name), being quite small, was unable to reach the nest until it had been well trampled upon and broken and the insects had made a counter charge with such vigor as to repulse and scatter our numbers in every direction. However, he evidently did not want to retreat without any honors; so he bravely jumped upon the nest and yelled:

"I, the brave Little Wound, to-day kill the only fierce enemy!"

So he bravely jumped upon the nest.

Scarcely were the last words uttered when he screamed as if stabbed to the heart. One of his older companions shouted:

"Dive into the water! Run! Dive into the water!" for there was a lake near by. This advice he obeyed.

When we had reassembled and were indulging in our mimic dance, Little Wound was not allowed to dance. He was considered not to be in existence—he had been killed by our enemies, the Bee tribe. Poor little fellow! His swollen face was sad and ashamed as he sat on a fallen log and watched the dance. Although he might well have styled himself one of the noble dead who had died for their country, yet he was not unmindful that he had screamed, and this weakness would be apt to recur to him many times in the future.

We had some quiet plays which we alternated with the more severe and warlike ones. Among them were throwing wands and snow-arrows. In the winter we coasted much. We had no "double-rippers" or toboggans, but six or seven of the long ribs of a buffalo, fastened together at the larger end, answered all practical purposes. Sometimes a strip of bass-wood bark, four feet long and about six inches wide, was used with considerable skill. We stood on one end and held the other, using the slippery inside of the bark for the outside, and thus coasting down long hills with remarkable speed.

The spinning of tops was one of the all-absorbing winter sports. We made our tops of heart-shaped wood, horn or bone. We whipped them with a long thong of buckskin. The handle was a stick about a foot long and sometimes we whittled the stick to make it spoon-shaped at one end.

We played games with these tops—two to fifty boys at one time. Each whips his top until it hums; then one takes the lead and the rest follow in a sort of obstacle race. The top must spin all the way through. There were bars of snow over which we must pilot our top in the spoon end of our whip; then again we would toss it in the air on to another open spot of ice or smooth snow-crust from twenty to fifty paces away. The top that holds out the longest is the winner.

Once when Hakadah was less than seven years old, he and a friend got caught in a swift and dangerous river current. Hakadah said:

. . . I can say now that I would rather ride on a swift bronco any day than try to stay on and steady a short log in a river. I never knew how we managed to prevent a shipwreck on that voyage and to reach the shore.

We had many curious wild pets. There were young foxes, bears, wolves, raccoons, fawns, buffalo calves and birds of all kinds, tamed by various boys. My pets were different at different times, but I particularly remember one. I once had a grizzly bear for a pet, and so far as he and I were concerned, our relations were charming and very close. But I hardly know whether he made more enemies for me or I for him. It was his habit to treat every boy unmercifully who injured me.

5

AN INDIAN BOY'S TRAINING

Very early, the Indian boy assumed the task of preserving and transmitting the legends of his ancestors and his race. Almost every evening a myth, or a true story of some deed done in the past, was narrated by one of the parents or grand-parents, while the boy listened with parted lips and glistening eyes. On the following evening, he was usually required to repeat it. If he was not an apt scholar, he struggled long with his task; but, as a rule, the Indian boy is a good listener and has a good memory, so that the stories were tolerably well mastered. The household became his audience, by which he was alternately criticized and applauded.

This sort of teaching at once enlightens the boy's mind and stimulates his ambition. His conception of his own future career becomes a vivid and irresistible force. Whatever there is for him to learn must be learned; whatever qualifications are necessary to a truly great man he must seek at any expense of danger and hardship. Such was the feeling of the imaginative and brave young Indian. It became apparent to him in early life that he must accustom himself to rove alone and not to fear or dislike the impression of solitude.

It seems to be a popular idea that all the characteristic skill of the Indian is instinctive and hereditary. This is a mistake. All the stoicism and patience of the Indian are acquired traits, and continual practice alone makes him master of the art of wood-craft. Physical training and dieting were not neglected. I remember that I was not allowed to have beef soup or any warm drink. The soup was for the old men. General rules for the young were never to take their food very hot, nor to drink much water.

My uncle, who educated me up to the age of fifteen years, was a strict disciplinarian and a good teacher. When I left the teepee in the morning, he would say: "Hakadah, look closely to everything you see"; and at evening, on my return, he used often to catechize me for an hour or so.

"On which side of the trees is the lighter-colored bark? On which side do they have most regular branches?"

It was his custom to let me name all the new birds that I had seen during the day. I would name them according to the color or the shape of the bill or their song or the appearance and locality of the nest—in fact, anything about the bird that impressed me as characteristic. I made many ridiculous errors, I must admit. He then usually informed me of the correct name. Occasionally I made a hit and this he would warmly commend.

He went much deeper into this science when I was a little older, that is, about the age of eight or nine years. He would say, for instance:

"How do you know that there are fish in yonder lake?"

"Because they jump out of the water for flies at midday."

He would smile at my prompt but superficial reply.

"What do you think of the little pebbles grouped together under the shallow water? and what made the pretty curved marks in the sandy bottom and the little sand-banks? Where do you find the fish-eating birds? Have the inlet and the outlet of a lake anything to do with the question?"

He did not expect a correct reply at once to all the questions that he put to me on these occasions, but he meant to make me observant and a good student of nature.

"Hakadah," he would say to me, "you ought to follow the example of the shunktokecha (wolf). Even when he is surprised and runs for his life, he will pause to take one more look at you before he enters his final retreat. So you must take a second look at everything you see.

"It is better to view animals unobserved. I have been a witness to their courtships and their quarrels and have learned many of their secrets in this way. I was once the unseen spectator of a thrilling battle between a pair of grizzly bears and three buffaloes—a rash act for the bears, for it was in the moon of strawberries, when the buffaloes sharpen and polish their horns for bloody contests among themselves.

Hakadah's uncle taught him how to hunt many animals, even grizzly bears.

"In hunting," he would resume, "you will be guided by the habits of the animal you seek. Remember that a moose stays in swampy or low land or between high mountains near a spring or lake, for thirty to sixty days at a time. Most large game moves about continually, except the doe in the spring; it is then a very easy matter to find her with the fawn. Conceal yourself in a convenient place as soon as you observe any signs of the presence of either, and then call with your birchen doe-caller.

"Whichever one hears you first will soon appear in your neighborhood. But you must be very watchful, or you may be made a fawn of by a large wild-cat. They understand the characteristic call of the doe perfectly well.

"When you have any difficulty with a bear or a wild-cat—that is, if the creature shows any signs of attacking you—you must make him fully understand that you have seen him and are aware of his intentions. If you are not well equipped for a pitched battle, the only way to make him retreat is to take a long sharp-pointed pole for a spear and rush toward him. No wild beast will face this unless he is cornered and already wounded. These fierce beasts are generally afraid of the common weapon of the larger animals,—the horns,—and if these are very long and sharp, they dare not risk an open fight.

"There is one exception to this rule—the gray wolf will attack fiercely when very hungry. But their courage depends upon their numbers; in this they are like white men. One wolf or two will never attack a man. They will stampede a herd of buffaloes in order to get at the calves; they will rush upon a herd of antelopes, for these are helpless; but they are always careful about attacking man."

Of this nature were the instructions of my uncle, who was widely known at that time as among the greatest hunters of his tribe.

All boys were expected to endure hardship without complaint. In savage warfare, a young man must, of course, be an athlete and used to undergoing all sorts of privations. He must be able to go without food and water for two or three days without displaying any weakness, or to run for a day and a night without any rest. He must be able to traverse a pathless and wild country without losing his way either in the day or night time. He cannot refuse to do any of these things if he aspires to be a warrior.

Sometimes my uncle would waken me very early in the morning and challenge me to fast with him all day. I had to accept the challenge. We blackened our faces with charcoal, so that every boy in the village would know that I was fasting for the day. Then the little tempters would make my life a misery until the merciful sun hid behind the western hills.

I can scarcely recall the time when my stern teacher began to give sudden war-whoops over my head in the morning while I was sound asleep. He expected me to leap up with perfect presence of mind, always ready to grasp a weapon of some sort and to give a shrill whoop in reply.

If Hakadah was sleepy or startled, his uncle would ridicule him.

Often he would vary these tactics by shooting off his gun just outside of the lodge while I was yet asleep, at the same time giving blood-curdling yells. After a time I became used to this.

When Indians went upon the war-path, it was their custom to try the new warriors thoroughly before coming to an engagement. For instance, when they were near a hostile camp, they would select the novices to go after the water and make them do all sorts of things to prove their courage. In accordance with this idea, my uncle used to send me off after water when we camped after dark in a strange place. Perhaps the country was full of wild beasts, and, for aught I knew, there might be scouts from hostile bands of Indians lurking in that very neighborhood.

Yet I never objected, for that would show cowardice. I picked my way through the woods, dipped my pail in the water and hurried back, always careful to make as little noise as a cat. Being only a boy, my heart would leap at every crackling of a dry twig or distant hooting of an owl, until, at last, I reached our teepee. Then my uncle would perhaps say: "Ah, Hakadah, you are a thorough warrior!" empty out the precious contents of the pail, and order me to go a second time.

Imagine how I felt! But I wished to be a brave man as much as a white boy desires to be a great lawyer or even President of the United States. Silently I would take the pail and endeavor to retrace my foot-steps in the dark.

With all this, our manners and morals were not neglected. I was made to respect the adults and especially the aged. I was not allowed to join in their discussions, nor even to speak in their presence, unless requested to do so. Indian etiquette was very strict, and among the requirements was that of avoiding the direct address. A term of relationship or some title of courtesy was commonly used instead of the personal name by those who wished to show respect. We were taught generosity to the poor.

Hakadah learned the traditional religion of his people.

6

THE BOY HUNTER

There was almost as much difference between the Indian boys who were brought up on the open prairies and those of the woods, as between city and country boys. The hunting of the prairie boys was limited and their knowledge of natural history imperfect. They were, as a rule, good riders, but in all-round physical development much inferior to the red men of the forest.

Our hunting varied with the season of the year, and the nature of the country which was for the time our home. Our chief weapon was the bow and arrows, and perhaps, if we were lucky, a knife was possessed by someone in the crowd. In the olden times, knives and hatchets were made from bone and sharp stones.

For fire we used a flint with a spongy piece of dry wood and a stone to strike with. Another way of starting fire was for several of the boys to sit down in a circle and rub two pieces of dry, spongy wood together, one after another, until the wood took fire.

We hunted in company a great deal, though it was a common thing for a boy to set out for the woods quite alone, and he usually enjoyed himself fully as much. Our game consisted mainly of small birds, rabbits, squirrels and grouse. Fishing, too, occupied much of our time. We hardly ever passed a creek or a pond without searching for some signs of fish. When fish were present, we always managed to get some. Fishlines were made of wild hemp, sinew or horse-hair. We either caught fish with lines, snared or speared them, or shot them with bow and arrows. In the fall we charmed them up to the surface by gently tickling them with a stick and quickly threw them out. We have sometimes dammed the brooks and driven the larger fish into a willow basket made for that purpose.

It was part of our hunting to find new and strange things in the woods. We examined the slightest sign of life; and if a bird had scratched the leaves off the ground, or a bear dragged up a root for his morning meal, we stopped to speculate on the time it was done.

If we saw a large old tree with some scratches on its bark, we concluded that a bear or some raccoons must be living there. In that case we did not go any nearer than was necessary, but later reported the incident at home. An old deer-track would at once bring on a warm discussion as to whether it was the track of a buck or a doe. Generally, at noon, we met and compared our game, noting at the same time the peculiar characteristics of everything we had killed. It was not merely a hunt, for we combined with it the study of animal life. We also kept strict account of our game, and thus learned who were the best shots among the boys.

I am sorry to say that we were merciless toward the birds. We often took their eggs and their young ones. My brother Chatanna and I once had a disagreeable adventure while bird-hunting. We were accustomed to catch in our hands young ducks and geese during the summer, and while doing this we happened to find a crane's nest. Of course, we were delighted with our good luck. But, as it was already midsummer, the young cranes—two in number—were rather large and they were a little way from the nest; we also observed that the two old cranes were in a swampy place near by; but, as it was moulting-time, we did not suppose that they would venture on dry land. So we proceeded to chase the young birds; but they were fleet runners and it took us some time to come up with them.

Meanwhile, the parent birds had heard the cries of their little ones and come to their rescue. They were chasing us, while we followed the birds. It was really a perilous encounter! Our strong bows finally gained the victory in a hand-to-hand struggle with the angry cranes; but after that we hardly ever hunted a crane's nest. Almost all birds make some resistance when their eggs or young are taken, but they will seldom attack man fearlessly.

We used to climb large trees for birds of all kinds; but we never undertook to get young owls unless they were on the ground. The hooting owl especially is a dangerous bird to attack under these circumstances.

I was once trying to catch a yellow-winged woodpecker in its nest when my arm became twisted and lodged in the deep hole so that I could not get it out without the aid of a knife; but we were a long way from home and my only companion was a deaf-mute cousin of mine. I was about fifty feet up in the tree, in a very uncomfortable position, but I had to wait there for more than an hour before he brought me the knife with which I finally released myself.

Our devices for trapping small animals were rude, but they were often successful. For instance, we used to gather up a peck or so of large, sharp-pointed burrs and scatter them in the rabbit's furrow-like path. In the morning, we would find the little fellow sitting quietly in his tracks, unable to move, for the burrs stuck to his feet.

The boys also enjoyed snaring rabbits and grouse.

Perhaps the most enjoyable of all was the chipmunk hunt. We killed these animals at any time of year, but the special time to hunt them was in March. After the first thaw, the chipmunks burrow a hole through the snow crust and make their first appearance for the season. Sometimes as many as fifty will come together and hold a social reunion. These gatherings occur early in the morning, from daybreak to about nine o'clock.

We boys learned this, among other secrets of nature, and got our blunt-headed arrows together in good season for the chipmunk expedition.

7

EVENING IN THE LODGE

I had been skating on that part of the lake where there was an overflow, and came home somewhat cold. I cannot say just how cold it was, but it must have been intensely so, for the trees were cracking all about me like pistol-shots. I did not mind, because I was wrapped up in my buffalo robe with the hair inside, and a wide leather belt held it about my loins. My skates were nothing more than strips of basswood bark bound upon my feet.

I had taken off my frozen moccasins and put on dry ones in their places.

"Where have you been and what have you been doing?" Uncheedah asked as she placed before me some roast venison in a wooden bowl. "Did you see any tracks of moose or bear?"

"No, grandmother, I have only been playing at the

lower end of the lake. I have something to ask you," I said, eating my dinner and supper together with all the relish of a hungry boy who has been skating in the cold for half a day.

"I found this feather, grandmother, and I could not make out what tribe wear feathers in that shape."

"Ugh, I am not a man; you had better ask your uncle. Besides, you should know it yourself by this time. You are now old enough to think about eagle feathers."

I felt mortified by this reminder of my ignorance. It seemed a reflection on me that I was not ambitious enough to have found all such matters out before.

"Uncle, you will tell me, won't you?" I said, in an appealing tone.

"I am surprised, my boy, that you should fail to recognize this feather. It is a Cree medicine feather, and not a warrior's."

"Then," I said, with much embarrassment, "you had better tell me again, uncle, the language of the feathers. I have really forgotten it all."

The day was now gone; the moon had risen; but the cold had not lessened, for the trunks of the trees were still snapping all around our teepee, which was lighted and warmed by the immense logs which Uncheedah's industry had provided. My uncle, White Footprint, now undertook to explain to me the significance of the eagle's feather.

"The eagle is the most war-like bird," he began, "and the most kingly of all birds; besides, his feathers are unlike any others, and these are the reasons why they are used by our people to signify deeds of bravery.

White Footprint explained to Hakadah how warriors earned feathers in battle.

"Tell me, uncle, whether it would be proper for me to wear any feathers at all if I have never gone upon the war-path."

"You could wear any other kind of feathers, but not an eagle's," replied my uncle, "although sometimes one is worn on great occasions by the child of a noted man, to indicate the father's dignity and position."

The fire had gone down somewhat, so I pushed the embers together and wrapped my robe more closely about me. Now and then the ice on the lake would burst with a loud report like thunder. Uncheedah was busy re-stringing one of uncle's old snow-shoes.

There were two different kinds that he wore; one with a straight toe and long; the other shorter and with an upturned toe. She had one of the shoes fastened toe down, between sticks driven into the ground, while she put in some new strings and tightened the others. Aunt Four Stars was beading a new pair of moccasins.

Wabeda, the dog, the companion of my boyhood days, was in trouble because he insisted upon bringing his extra bone into the teepee, while Uncheedah was determined that he should not. I sympathized with him, because I saw the matter as he did. If he should bury it in the snow outside, I knew Shunktokecha (the coyote) would surely steal it. I knew just how anxious Wabeda was about his bone. It was a fat bone—I mean a bone of a fat deer; and all Indians know how much better they are than the other kind.

Wabeda always hated to see a good thing go to waste. His eyes spoke words to me, for he and I had been friends for a long time. When I was afraid of anything in the woods, he would get in front of me at once and gently wag his tail. He always made it a point to look directly in my face. His kind, large eyes gave me a thousand assurances. When I was perplexed, he would hang about me until he understood the situation. Many times I believed he saved my life by uttering the dog word in time.

I believe that Charles A. Eastman is talking about his dog barking.

Most animals, even the dangerous grizzly, do not care to be seen when the two-legged kind and his dog are about. When I feared a surprise by a bear or a gray wolf, I would say to Wabeda: "Now, my dog, give your war-whoop!" and immediately he would sit up on his haunches and bark "to beat the band," as you white boys say. When a bear or wolf heard the noise, he would be apt to retreat.

Sometimes I helped Wabeda and gave a war-whoop of my own. This drove the deer away as well, but it relieved my mind.

When he appealed to me on this occasion, therefore, I said: "Come, my dog, let us bury your bone so that no Shunktokecha will take it."

He appeared satisfied with my suggestion, so we went out together.

We dug in the snow and buried our bone wrapped up in a piece of old blanket, partly burned; then we covered it up again with snow. We knew that the coyote would not touch anything burnt. I did not put it up a tree because Wabeda always objected to that, and I made it a point to consult his wishes whenever I could.

I came in and Wabeda followed me with two short

rib bones in his mouth. Apparently he did not care to risk those delicacies.

"There," exclaimed Uncheedah, "you still insist upon bringing in some sort of bone!" but I begged her to let him gnaw them inside because it was so cold. Having been granted this privilege, he settled himself at my back and I became absorbed in some specially nice arrows that uncle was making.

"Oh, uncle, you must put on three feathers to all of them so that they can fly straight," I suggested.

"Yes, but if there are only two feathers, they will fly faster," he answered.

"Woow!" Wabeda uttered his suspicions.

"Woow!" he said again, and rushed for the entrance of the teepee. He kicked me over as he went and scattered the burning embers.

"En na he na!" Uncheedah exclaimed, but he was already outside.

"Wow, wow, wow! Wow, wow, wow!"

A deep guttural voice answered him. Out I rushed with my bow and arrows in my hand.

"Come, uncle, come! A big cinnamon bear!" I shouted as I emerged from the teepee.

Uncle sprang out, and in a moment he had sent a swift arrow through the bear's heart. The animal fell dead. He had just begun to dig up Wabeda's bone, when the dog's quick ear had heard the sound.

"Ah, uncle, Wabeda and I ought to have at least a little eaglet's feather for this! I too sent my small arrow into the bear before he fell," I exclaimed. "But I thought all bears ought to be in their lodges in the winter time. What was this one doing at this time of the year and night?"

"Well," said my uncle, "I will tell you. Among the tribes, some are naturally lazy. The cinnamon bear is the lazy one of his tribe. He alone sleeps out of doors in the winter, and because he has not a warm bed, he is soon hungry. Sometimes he lives in the hollow trunk of a tree, where he has made a bed of dry grass; but when the night is very cold, like to-night, he has to move about to keep himself from freezing, and as he prowls around, he gets hungry."

We dragged the huge carcass within our lodge. "Oh, what nice claws he has, uncle!" I exclaimed eagerly. "Can I have them for my necklace?"

"It is only the old medicine-men who wear them regularly. The son of a great warrior who has killed a grizzly may wear them upon a public occasion," he explained.

"And you are just like my father and are considered the best hunter among the Santees and Sissetons. You have killed many grizzlies, so that no one can object to my bear's-claw necklace," I said appealingly.

Many native nations are comprised of many bands or sub-nations. Hakadah's family was in the Santee Sioux band.

White Footprint smiled. "My boy, you shall have them," he said, "but it is always better to earn them yourself." He cut the claws off carefully for my use.

"Tell me, uncle, whether you could wear these claws all the time?" I asked.

"Yes, I am entitled to wear them, but they are so heavy and uncomfortable," he replied, with a superior air.

At last the bear had been skinned and dressed and we all resumed our usual places. Uncheedah was particularly pleased to have some more fat for her cooking.

"Now, grandmother, tell me the story of the bear's fat. I shall be so happy if you will," I begged.

"It is a good story and it is true. You should know it by heart and gain a lesson from it," she replied. "It was in the forests of Minnesota, in the country that now belongs to the Ojibways. From the Bedawakanton Sioux village a young married couple went into the woods to get fresh venison. The snow was deep; the ice was thick. Far away in the woods they pitched their lonely teepee. The young man was a well-known hunter and his wife a good maiden of the village.

"He hunted entirely on snowshoes, because the snow was very deep. His wife had to wear snowshoes too, to get to the spot where they pitched their tent. It was thawing the day they went out, so their path was distinct after the freeze came again.

"The young man killed many deer and bears. His wife was very busy curing the meat and trying out the fat while he was away hunting each day. In the evenings she kept on trying the fat. He sat on one side of the teepee and she on the other.

"One evening, she had just lowered a kettle of fat to cool, and as she looked into the hot fat she saw the face of an Ojibway scout looking down at them through the smoke-hole. She said nothing, nor did she betray herself in any way.

"After a little she said to her husband in a natural voice: 'Marpeetopah, some one is looking at us through the smoke-hole, and I think it is an enemy's scout.'

This was the beginning of a terrible battle between the Dakota people and the Ojibwe. Many on both sides died in the battle.

It was after this that the Sioux moved to the Mississippi river."

I was sleepy by this time and I rolled myself up in my buffalo robe and fell asleep.

8

WHEN WINONA
WAS A LITTLE GIRL

"Chinto, wéyanna! Yes, indeed; she is a real little woman," declares the old grandmother, as she receives and critically examines the tiny bit of humanity.

There is no remark as to the color of its hair or eyes, both so black as almost to be blue, but the old woman scans sharply the delicate profile of the baby face.

"Ah, she has the nose of her ancestors! Lips thin as a leaf, and eyes bright as stars in midwinter!" she exclaims, as she passes on the furry bundle to the other grandmother for her inspection.

"Tokee! she is pretty enough to win a twinkle from the evening star," remarks that smiling personage.

"And what shall her name be?"

"Winona, the First-born, of course. That is hers by right of birth."

"Still, it may not fit her. One must prove herself worthy in order to retain that honorable name."

"Ugh," retorts the first grandmother, "she can at least bear it on probation!"

"Tosh, tosh," the other assents.

These were the first steps in the naming of this new baby girl.

Presently she is folded into a soft white doeskin, well lined with the loose down of cattails, and snugly laced into an upright oaken cradle, the front of which is a richly embroidered buckskin bag, with porcupine quills and deer's hoofs suspended from its profuse fringes. This gay cradle is strapped upon the second grandmother's back, and that dignitary walks off with the newcomer.

The grandmother hung the baby's cradleboard from a tree.

The baby girl is called Winona for some months, when the medicine-man is summoned and requested to name publicly the first-born daughter of Chetonska, the White Hawk; but not until he has received a present of a good pony with a finely painted buffalo-robe. It is usual to confer another name besides that of the "First-born," which may be resumed later if the maiden proves worthy. The name Winona implies much of honor. It means charitable, kind, helpful; all that an eldest sister should be!

A herald goes around the ring of lodge homes announcing in a singsong voice the naming of the baby. He invites everyone to a feast in honor of the event. The family gives gifts to the poor and to the old people.

Winona has only just walked, and this fact is also announced with additional gifts. A well-born child is ever before the tribal eye and in the tribal ear, as every little step in its progress toward manhood or womanhood—the first time of walking or swimming, first shot with bow and arrow (if a boy), first pair of moccasins made (if a girl)—is announced publicly with feasting and the giving of presents.

So Winona receives her individual name of Tatiyopa, or Her Door. It is symbolic, like most Indian names, and implies that the door of the bearer is hospitable and her home attractive.

The two grandmothers, who have carried the little maiden upon their backs, now tell and sing to her by turns all the legends of their most noted female ancestors, . . .

The grandmothers tell stories about the baby's female ancestors all the way down to their own mothers.

All their lullabies are feminine, and designed to impress upon her tender mind the life and duties of her sex.

As soon as she is old enough to play with dolls, she plays mother in all seriousness and gravity. She is dressed like a miniature woman (and her dolls are clad likewise), in garments of doeskin to her ankles, adorned with long fringes, embroidered with porcupine quills, and dyed with root dyes in various colors. Her little blanket or robe, with which she shyly drapes or screens her head and shoulders, is the skin of a buffalo calf or a deer, soft, white, embroidered on the smooth side, and often with the head and hoofs left on.

"You must never forget, my little daughter, that you are a woman like myself. Do always those things that you see me do," her mother often admonishes her.

Even the language of the Sioux has its feminine dialect, and the tiny girl would be greatly abashed were it ever needful to correct her for using a masculine termination.

This mother makes for her little daughter a miniature copy of every rude tool that she uses in her daily tasks. There is a little scraper of elk-horn to scrape raw-hides preparatory to tanning them, another scraper of a different shape for tanning, bone knives, and stone mallets for pounding choke-cherries and jerked meat.

While her mother is bending over a large buffalo-hide stretched and pinned upon the ground, standing upon it and scraping off the fleshy portion as nimbly as a carpenter shaves a board with his plane, Winona, at five years of age, stands upon a corner of the great hide and industriously scrapes away with her tiny instrument. When the mother stops to sharpen her tool, the little woman always sharpens hers also. Perhaps there is water to be fetched in bags made from the dried pericardium of an animal; the girl brings some in a smaller water-bag. When her mother goes for wood she carries one or two sticks on her back. She pitches her play teepee to form an exact copy of her mother's. Her little belongings are nearly all practical, and her very play is real!

9

WINONA BECOMES A YOUNG MAIDEN

Many years have passed since Winona was a baby. Charles Eastman began the chapter with the words of a Sioux Love Song. In the song, the man the girl loves has died while seeking honor. She asks him if he could not remember the one who weeps at home.

The sky is blue overhead, peeping through window-like openings in a roof of green leaves. Right between a great pine and a birch tree their soft doeskin shawls are spread, and there sit two Sioux maidens amid their fineries—variously colored porcupine quills for embroidery laid upon sheets of thin birch-bark, and moccasin tops worked in colors like autumn leaves. It is Winona and her friend Miniyata.

They have arrived at the period during which the young girl is carefully secluded from her brothers and cousins and future lovers, and retires, as it were, into the nunnery of the woods, behind a veil of thick foliage. Thus she is expected to develop her womanly qualities. In meditation and solitude, entirely alone or with a chosen companion of her own sex and age, she gains a secret strength, as she studies the art of womanhood from nature herself.

Winona and Miniyata practice their traditional dance. Each wears a wreath of wildflowers on her head. They dance with slow steps around a white birch tree while singing traditional songs.

Now upon the lake that stretches blue to the eastward there appears a distant canoe, a mere speck, no bigger than a bird far off against the shining sky.

"See the lifting of the paddles!" exclaims Winona.

"Like the leaping of a trout upon the water!" suggests Miniyata.

"I hope they will not discover us, yet I would like to know who they are," remarks the other, innocently.

The birch canoe approaches swiftly, with two young men plying the light cedar paddles.

The girls now settle down to their needle-work, quite as if they had never laughed or danced or woven garlands, bending over their embroidery in perfect silence. Surely they would not wish to attract attention, for the two sturdy young warriors have already landed.

They pick up the canoe and lay it well up on the bank, out of sight. Then one procures a strong pole. They lift a buck deer from the canoe—not a mark upon it, save for the bullet wound; the deer looks as if it were sleeping! They tie the hind legs together and the fore legs also and carry it between them on the pole.

Quickly and cleverly they do all this; and now they start forward and come unexpectedly upon the maidens' retreat! They pause for an instant in mute apology, but the girls smile their forgiveness, and the youths hurry on toward the village.

Winona has now attended her first maidens' feast and is considered eligible to marriage.

When a young man speaks to a maiden, she doesn't have to answer him unless she wants to.

It was no disgrace to the chief's daughter in the old days to work with her hands. Indeed, their standard of worth was the willingness to work, but not for the sake of accumulation, only in order to give. Winona has learned to prepare skins, to remove the hair and tan the skin of a deer so that it may be made into moccasins within three days. She has a bone tool for each stage of the conversion of the stiff rawhide into velvety leather. She has been taught the art of painting tents and rawhide cases, and the manufacture of garments of all kinds.

Generosity is a trait that is highly developed in the Sioux woman. She makes many moccasins and other articles of clothing for her male relatives, or for any who are not well provided. She loves to see her brother the best dressed among the young men, and the moccasins especially of a young brave are the pride of his womankind.

Her own person is neatly attired, but ordinarily with great simplicity.

Charles A. Eastman describes a maiden's doeskin gown with its wide, flowing sleeves.

Her moccasins are plain; her leggins close-fitting and not as high as her brother's. She parts her smooth, jet-black hair in the middle and plaits it in two. In the old days she used to do it in one plait wound around with wampum. Her ornaments, sparingly worn, are beads, elks' teeth, and a touch of red paint. No feathers are worn by the woman, unless in a sacred dance. She is supposed to be always occupied with some feminine pursuit or engaged in some social affair, which also is strictly feminine as a rule.

Charles A. Eastman talks about how modest the girls are and about the fun times they have with each other.

In summer, swimming and playing in the water is a favorite amusement. She even imitates with the soles of her feet the peculiar, resonant sound that the beaver makes with her large, flat tail upon the surface of the water. She is a graceful swimmer, keeping the feet together and waving them backward and forward like the tail of a fish.

Nearly all her games are different from those of the men. She has a sport of wand-throwing, which develops fine muscles of the shoulder and back. The wands are about eight feet long, and taper gradually from an inch and a half to half an inch in diameter. Some of them are artistically made, with heads of bone and horn, so that it is remarkable to what a distance they may be made to slide over the ground. In the feminine game of ball, which is something like "shinny," the ball is driven with curved sticks between two goals. It is played with from two or three to a hundred on a side, and a game between two bands or villages is a picturesque event.

A common indoor diversion is the "deer's foot" game, played with six deer hoofs on a string, ending in a bone or steel awl. The object is to throw it in such a way as to catch one or more hoofs on the point of the awl, a feat which requires no little dexterity. Another is played with marked plum-stones in a bowl, which are thrown like dice and count according to the side that is turned uppermost.

A young man named Matosapa has noticed Winona and hopes that she will marry him. Many young men find wives in midsummer when the Santee Sioux get together for reunions and festivals. Young men usually spend their time with a close male friend. Young women spend time with a close female friend. When the young man and maiden who are interested in one another meet, their friends are with them.

At the sound of the drum on summer evenings, dances are begun within the circular rows of teepees, but without the circle the young men promenade in pairs. Each provides himself with the plaintive flute and plays the simple cadences of his people, while his person is completely covered with his fine robe, so that he cannot be recognized by the passer-by. At every pause in the melody he gives his yodel-like love-call, to which the girls respond with their musical, sing-song laughter.

Matosapa has improved every opportunity, until Winona has at last shyly admitted her willingness to listen. For a whole year he has been compelled at intervals to repeat the story of his love. Through the autumn hunting of the buffalo and the long, cold winter he often presents her kinsfolk with his game.

At the next midsummer the parents on both sides are made acquainted with the betrothal, and they at once begin preparations for the coming wedding. Provisions and delicacies of all kinds are laid aside for a feast. Matosapa's sisters and his girl cousins are told of the approaching event, and they too prepare for it, since it is their duty to dress or adorn the bride with garments made by their own hands.

The bride is ceremoniously delivered to her husband's people, together with presents of rich clothing, collected from all her clan, which she afterward distributes among her new relations. Winona is carried in a travois handsomely decorated, and is received with equal ceremony.

10

MIDSUMMER FEAST & BALLGAME

The Wahpetonwan village on the banks of the Minnesota river was alive with the newly-arrived guests and the preparations for the coming event. Meat of wild game had been put away with much care during the previous fall in anticipation of this feast. There was wild rice and the choicest of dried venison that had been kept all winter, as well as freshly dug turnips, ripe berries and an abundance of fresh meat.

Along the edge of the woods the teepees were pitched in groups or semi-circles, each band distinct from the others. The teepee of Mankato or Blue Earth was pitched in a conspicuous spot. Just over the entrance was painted in red and yellow a picture of a pipe, and directly opposite this the rising sun. The painting was symbolic of welcome and good will to men under the bright sun.

A meeting was held to appoint some "medicine-man" to make the balls that were to be used in the lacrosse contest; and presently the herald announced that this honor had been conferred upon old Chankpee-yuhah, or "Keeps the Club," while every other man of his profession was disappointed.

Towards evening he appeared in the circle, leading by the hand a boy about four years old. Closely the little fellow observed every motion of the man; nothing escaped his vigilant black eyes, which seemed constantly to grow brighter and larger.

The little boy's glossy black hair was plaited and wound around his head.

He wore a bit of swan's down in each ear, which formed a striking contrast with the child's complexion. Further than this, the boy was painted according to the fashion of the age. He held in his hands a miniature bow and arrows.

The medicine-man drew himself up in an admirable attitude, and proceeded to make his short speech:

"Wahpetonwans, you boast that you run down the elk; you can outrun the Ojibways. Before you all, I dedicate to you this red ball. Kaposias, you claim that no one has a lighter foot than you; you declare that you can endure running a whole day without water. To you I dedicate this black ball. Either you or the Leaf-Dwellers will have to drop your eyes and bow your head when the game is over. I wish to announce that if the Wahpetonwans should win, this little warrior shall bear the name Ohiyesa (winner) through life; but if the Light Lodges should win, let the name be given to any child appointed by them."

The ground selected for the great game was on a narrow strip of land between a lake and the river. It was about three quarters of a mile long and a quarter of a mile in width. The spectators had already ranged themselves all along the two sides, as well as at the two ends, which were somewhat higher than the middle. The soldiers appointed to keep order furnished much of the entertainment of the day. They painted artistically and tastefully, according to the Indian fashion, not only their bodies but also their ponies and clubs. They were so strict in enforcing the laws that no one could venture with safety within a few feet of the limits of the field.

Now all of the minor events and feasts, occupying several days' time, had been observed. Heralds on ponies' backs announced that all who intended to participate in the final game were requested to repair to the ground; also that if any one bore a grudge against another, he was implored to forget his ill-feeling until the contest should be over.

The most powerful men were stationed at the halfway ground, while the fast runners were assigned to the back. It was an impressive spectacle, a fine collection of agile forms, almost stripped of garments and painted in wild imitation of the rainbow and sunset sky on human canvas. Some had undertaken to depict the Milky Way across their tawny bodies, and one or two made a bold attempt to reproduce the lightning. Others contented themselves with painting the figure of some fleet animal or swift bird on their muscular chests.

At the middle of the ground were stationed four immense men, magnificently formed. A fifth approached this group, paused a moment, and then threw his head back, gazed up into the sky in the manner of a cock and gave a smooth, clear operatic tone. Instantly the little black ball went up between the two middle rushers, in the midst of yells, cheers and war-whoops. Both men endeavored to catch it in the air; but alas! each interfered with the other; then the guards on each side rushed upon them. For a time, a hundred lacrosse sticks vied with each other, and the wriggling human flesh and paint were all one could see through the cloud of dust. Suddenly there shot swiftly through the air toward the south, toward the Kaposias' goal, the ball. There was a general cheer from their adherents, which echoed back from the white cliff on the opposite side of the Minnesota.

As the ball flew through the air, two adversaries were ready to receive it. The Kaposia quickly met the ball, but failed to catch it in his netted bag, for the other had swung his up like a flash. Thus it struck the ground, but had no opportunity to bound up when a Wahpeton pounced upon it like a cat and slipped out of the grasp of his opponents. A mighty cheer thundered through the air.

The warrior who had undertaken to pilot the little sphere was risking much, for he must dodge a host of Kaposias before he could gain any ground. He was alert and agile; now springing like a panther, now leaping like a deer over a stooping opponent who tried to seize him around the waist. Every opposing player was upon his heels, while those of his own side did all in their power to clear the way for him. But it was all in vain. He only gained fifty paces.

Thus the game went. First one side, then the other would gain an advantage, and then it was lost, until the herald proclaimed that it was time to change the ball. No victory was in sight for either side.

After a few minutes' rest, the game was resumed. The red ball was now tossed in the air in the usual way. No sooner had it descended than one of the rushers caught it and away it went northward; again it was fortunate, for it was advanced by one of the same side. The scene was now one of the wildest excitement and confusion. At last, the northward flight of the ball was checked for a moment and a desperate struggle ensued.

The ball had not been allowed to come to the surface since it reached this point, for there were more than a hundred men who scrambled for it. Suddenly a warrior shot out of the throng like the ball itself! Then some of the players shouted: "Look out for Antelope!" But it was too late. The little sphere had already nestled into Antelope's palm and that fleetest of Wahpetons had thrown down his lacrosse stick and set a determined eye upon the northern goal.

Such a speed! He had cleared almost all the opponents' guards—there were but two more. These were exceptional runners of the Kaposias. As he approached them in his almost irresistible speed, every savage heart thumped louder in the Indian's dusky bosom. In another moment there would be a defeat for the Kaposias or a prolongation of the game. The two men, with a determined look approached their foe like two panthers prepared to spring; yet he neither slackened his speed nor deviated from his course. A crash—a mighty shout!—the two Kaposias collided, and the swift Antelope had won the laurels!

The turmoil and commotion at the victors' camp were indescribable. A few beats of a drum were heard, after which the criers hurried along the lines, announcing the last act to be performed at the camp of the "Leaf Dwellers."

The day had been a perfect one. Every event had been a success; and, as a matter of course, the old people were happy, for they largely profited by these occasions. Within the circle formed by the general assembly sat in a group the members of the common council. Blue Earth arose, and in a few appropriate and courteous remarks assured his guests that it was not selfishness that led his braves to carry off the honors of the last event, but that this was a friendly contest in which each band must assert its prowess.

In memory of this victory, the boy would now receive his name. A loud "Ho-o-o" of approbation reverberated from the edge of the forest upon the Minnesota's bank.

Half frightened, the little fellow was now brought into the circle, looking very much as if he were about to be executed. Cheer after cheer went up for the awe-stricken boy. Chankpee-yuhah, the medicine-man, proceeded to confer the name.

"Ohiyesa (or Winner) shall be thy name henceforth. Be brave, be patient and thou shalt always win! Thy name is Ohiyesa."

11

EARLIEST MEMORIES

Charles A. Eastman included the stories you have read so far in his book Indian Child Life. *The following stories are from one of his other books,* Indian Boyhood. *Some of the following stories are from the same time period he described in* Indian Child Life, *but they are so interesting that I thought you might enjoy these, too. As you remember, Eastman's mother died when he was still a baby and his father's mother took care of him.*

What boy would not be an Indian for a while when he thinks of the freest life in the world? This life was mine. Every day there was a real hunt. There was real game. Occasionally there was a medicine dance away off in the woods where no one could disturb us, in which the boys impersonated their elders, Brave Bull, Standing Elk, High Hawk, Medicine Bear, and the rest. They painted and imitated their fathers and grandfathers to the minutest detail, and accurately too, because they had seen the real thing all their lives.

We were not only good mimics but we were close students of nature. We studied the habits of animals just as you study your books.

Ohiyesa's people thought his mother was the handsomest woman in their nation. She had the luxuriant black hair and deep black eyes of her mother's family and the facial features of her father who was the American soldier Seth Eastman. Ohiyesa's mother was very ill. She held her baby tightly to her chest on her death bed and whispered to her mother-in-law, "I give you this boy for your own."

The woman to whom these words were spoken was below the average in stature, remarkably active for her age (she was then fully sixty), and possessed of as much goodness as intelligence.

Giving Ohiyesa into the care of her mother-in-law was a wise decision. She loved him and took good care of him.

My food was, at first, a troublesome question for my kind foster-mother. She cooked some wild rice and strained it, and mixed it with broth made from choice venison. She also pounded dried venison almost to a flour, and kept it in water till the nourishing juices were extracted, then mixed with it some pounded maize, which was browned before pounding. This soup of wild rice, pounded venison and maize was my main-stay.

My babyhood was full of interest and the beginnings of life's realities.

Even as a toddler, Ohiyesa was daring.

The value of the eagle feather as worn by the warrior had caught my eye. One day, when I was left alone, at scarcely two years of age, I took my uncle's war bonnet and plucked out all its eagle feathers to decorate my dog and myself. So soon the life that was about me had made its impress, and already I desired intensely to comply with all of its demands.

This is what happened one time while Ohiyesa was riding in his cradleboard.

This mode of travelling for children was possible only in the summer, and as the dogs were sometimes unreliable, the little ones were exposed to a certain amount of danger. For instance, whenever a train of dogs had been travelling for a long time, almost perishing with the heat and their heavy loads, a glimpse of water would cause them to forget all their responsibilities. Some of them, in spite of the screams of the women, would swim with their burdens into the cooling stream, and I was thus, on more than one occasion, made to partake of an unwilling bath.

Ohiyesa was a little over four years old when he became separated from his father and older brothers.

I must say a word in regard to the character of this uncle, my father's brother, who was my adviser and teacher for many years. He was a man about six feet two inches in height, very erect and broad-shouldered. He was known at that time as one of the best hunters and bravest warriors among the Sioux in British America, where he still lives, for to this day we have failed to persuade him to return to the United States.

He is a typical Indian—not handsome, but truthful and brave. He had a few simple principles from which he hardly ever departed. Some of these I shall describe when I speak of my early training.

It is wonderful that any children grew up through all the exposures and hardships that we suffered in those days! The frail teepee pitched anywhere, in the winter as well as in the summer, was all the protection that we had against cold and storms. I can recall times when we were snowed in and it was very difficult to get fuel. We were once three days without much fire and all of this time it stormed violently. There seemed to be no special anxiety on the part of our people; they rather looked upon all this as a matter of course, knowing that the storm would cease when the time came.

I could once endure as much cold and hunger as any of them; but now if I miss one meal or accidentally wet my feet, I feel it as much as if I had never lived in the manner I have described, when it was a matter of course to get myself soaking wet many a time. Even if there was plenty to eat, it was thought better for us to practice fasting sometimes; and hard exercise was kept up continually, both for the sake of health and to prepare the body for the extraordinary exertions that it might, at any moment, be required to undergo. In my own remembrance, my uncle used often to bring home a deer on his shoulder. The distance was sometimes considerable; yet he did not consider it any sort of a feat.

The usual custom with us was to eat only two meals a day and these were served at each end of the day. This rule was not invariable, however, for if there should be any callers, it was Indian etiquette to offer either tobacco or food, or both. The rule of two meals a day was more closely observed by the men—especially the younger men—than by the women and children. This was when the Indians recognized that a true manhood, one of physical activity and endurance, depends upon dieting and regular exercise.

12

UNCHEEDAH, MY GRANDMOTHER

As a motherless child, I always regarded my good grandmother as the wisest of guides and the best of protectors. It was not long before I began to realize her superiority to most of her contemporaries. This idea was not gained entirely from my own observation, but also from a knowledge of the high regard in which she was held by other women. Aside from her native talent and ingenuity, she was endowed with a truly wonderful memory. No other midwife in her day and tribe could compete with her in skill and judgment. Her observations in practice were all preserved in her mind for reference, as systematically as if they had been written upon the pages of a note-book.

I distinctly recall one occasion when she took me with her into the woods in search of certain medicinal roots.

Ohiyesa questioned his grandmother about finding and digging plants for medicine. She told him:

"Some day Ohiyesa will be old enough to know the secrets of medicine; then I will tell him all. But if you should grow up to be a bad man, I must withhold these treasures from you and give them to your brother, for a medicine man must be a good and wise man. I hope Ohiyesa will be a great medicine man when he grows up. To be a great warrior is a noble ambition; but to be a mighty medicine man is a nobler!"

She said these things so thoughtfully and impressively that I cannot but feel and remember them even to this day.

Our native women gathered all the wild rice, roots, berries and fruits which formed an important part of our food. This was distinctively a woman's work. Uncheedah (grandmother) understood these matters perfectly, and it became a kind of instinct with her to know just where to look for each edible variety and at what season of the year. This sort of labor gave the Indian women every opportunity to observe and study Nature after their fashion; and in this Uncheedah was more acute than most of the men. The abilities of her boys were not all inherited from their father; indeed, the stronger family traits came obviously from her. She was a leader among the native women, and they came to her, not only for medical aid, but for advice in all their affairs.

In bravery she equaled any of the men. This trait, together with her ingenuity and alertness of mind, more than once saved her and her people from destruction. Once, when we were roaming over a region occupied by other tribes, and on a day when most of the men were out upon the hunt, a party of hostile Indians suddenly appeared. Although there were a few men left at home, they were taken by surprise at first and scarcely knew what to do, when this woman came forward and advanced alone to meet our foes. She had gone some distance when some of the men followed her. She met the strangers and offered her hand to them. They accepted her friendly greeting; and as a result of her brave act we were left unmolested and at peace.

Another story of her was related to me by my father. My grandfather, who was a noted hunter, often wandered away from his band in search of game. In this instance he had with him only his own family of three boys and his wife. One evening, when he returned from the chase, he found to his surprise that she had built a stockade around her teepee.

She had discovered the danger-sign in a single footprint, which she saw at a glance was not that of her husband, and she was also convinced that it was not the foot-print of a Sioux, from the shape of the moccasin. This ability to recognize footprints is general among the Indians, but more marked in certain individuals.

One day Ohiyesa's grandmother's dog warned her that five Ojibwe warriors were coming close. She was able to frighten them away.

I was not more than five or six years old when the Indian soldiers came one day and destroyed our large buffalo-skin teepee. It was charged that my uncle had hunted alone a large herd of buffaloes. This was not exactly true. He had unfortunately frightened a large herd while shooting a deer in the edge of the woods. However, it was customary to punish such an act severely, even though the offense was accidental.

When we were attacked by the police, I was playing in the teepee, and the only other person at home was Uncheedah. I had not noticed their approach, and when the war-cry was given by thirty or forty Indians with strong lungs, I thought my little world was coming to an end.

When these native soldiers/police came to punish Ohiyesa's uncle, they attacked their teepee.

I hardly know what I did, but I imagine it was just what any other little fellow would have done under like circumstances. My first clear realization of the situation was when Uncheedah had a dispute with the leader, claiming that the matter had not been properly investigated, and that none of the policemen had attained to a reputation in war which would justify them in touching her son's teepee. But alas! our poor dwelling was already an unrecognizable ruin; even the poles were broken into splinters.

The Indian women, after reaching middle age, are usually heavy and lack agility, but my grandmother was in this also an exception. She was fully sixty when I was born; and when I was seven years old she swam across a swift and wide stream, carrying me on her back, because she did not wish to expose me to accident in one of the clumsy round boats of bull-hide which were rigged up to cross the rivers which impeded our way, especially in the springtime. Her strength and endurance were remarkable. Even after she had attained the age of eighty-two, she one day walked twenty-five miles without appearing much fatigued.

I marvel now at the purity and elevated sentiment possessed by this woman, when I consider the customs and habits of her people at the time. When her husband died she was still comparatively a young woman—still active, clever and industrious. She was descended from a haughty chieftain of the "Dwellers among the Leaves." Although women of her age and position were held to be eligible to re-marriage, and she had several persistent suitors who were men of her own age and chiefs, yet she preferred to cherish in solitude the memory of her husband.

During a fight between the Santee Sioux and the Objibwe, Ohiyesa's uncle brought home two Ojibwe women as captives.

I was very small when my uncle brought home two Ojibway young women. In the fight in which they were captured, none of the Sioux war party had been killed; therefore they were sympathized with and tenderly treated by the Sioux women. They were apparently happy, although of course they felt deeply the losses sustained at the time of their capture, and they did not fail to show their appreciation of the kindnesses received at our hands.

As I recall now the remarks made by one of them at the time of their final release, they appear to me quite remarkable. They lived in my grandmother's family for two years, and were then returned to their people at a great peace council of the two nations. When they were about to leave my grandmother, the elder of the two sisters first embraced her, and then spoke somewhat as follows:

"You are a brave woman and a true mother. I understand now why your son so bravely conquered our band, and took my sister and myself captive. I hated him at first, but now I admire him, because he did just what my father, my brother or my husband would have done had they opportunity. He did even more. He saved us from the tomahawks of his fellow-warriors, and brought us to his home to know a noble and a brave woman.

"I shall never forget your many favors shown to us. But I must go. I belong to my tribe and I shall return to them. I will endeavor to be a true woman also, and to teach my boys to be generous warriors like your son."

Her sister chose to remain among the Sioux all her life, and she married one of our young men.

"I shall make the Sioux and the Ojibways," she said, "to be as brothers."

There are many other instances of intermarriage with captive women. The mother of the well-known Sioux chieftain, Wabashaw, was an Ojibway woman. I once knew a woman who was said to be a white captive. She was married to a noted warrior, and had a fine family of five boys. She was well accustomed to the Indian ways, and as a child I should not have suspected that she was white. The skins of these people became so sunburned and full of paint that it required a keen eye to distinguish them from the real Indians.

13

MOTHERS, FATHERS, AND CHILDREN

It is commonly supposed that there is no systematic education of their children among the aborigines of this country. Nothing could be farther from the truth.

Charles A. Eastman said that native nations were careful to pass down from one generation to the next what they believed was important for children to know.

The expectant parents conjointly bent all their efforts to the task of giving the new-comer the best they could gather from a long line of ancestors. A pregnant Indian woman would often choose one of the greatest characters of her family and tribe as a model for her child. This hero was daily called to mind. She would gather from tradition all of his noted deeds and daring exploits, rehearsing them to herself when alone. In order that the impression might be more distinct, she avoided company. She isolated herself as much as possible, and wandered in solitude, not thoughtlessly, but with an eye to the impress given by grand and beautiful scenery.

Parents and other adults in a baby's life talked about what kind of person he or she would be someday.

Those ideas which so fully occupied his mother's mind before his birth are now put into words by all about the child, who is as yet quite unresponsive to their appeals to his honor and ambition. He is called the future defender of his people, whose lives may depend upon his courage and skill. If the child is a girl, she is at once addressed as the future mother of a noble race.

14

PLAYMATES

Occasionally, we also played "white man." Our knowledge of the pale-face was limited, but we had learned that he brought goods whenever he came and that our people exchanged furs for his merchandise. We also knew that his complexion was pale, that he had short hair on his head and long hair on his face and that he wore coat, trousers, and hat, and did not patronize blankets in the daytime. This was the picture we had formed of the white man.

So we painted two or three of our number with white clay and put on them birchen hats which we sewed up for the occasion; fastened a piece of fur to their chins for a beard and altered their costumes as much as lay within our power. The white of the birch-bark was made to answer for their white shirts. Their merchandise consisted of sand for sugar, wild beans for coffee, dried leaves for tea, pulverized earth for gun-powder, pebbles for bullets and . . .

Ohiyesa said that they used clear water for the dangerous liquor that the white men sold them.

We traded for these goods with skins of squirrels, rabbits and small birds.

Chatanna was the brother with whom I passed much of my early childhood. From the time that I was old enough to play with boys, this brother was my close companion. He was a handsome boy, and an affectionate comrade. We played together, slept together and ate together; and as Chatanna was three years the older, I naturally looked up to him as to a superior.

Oesedah was a beautiful little character. She was my cousin, and four years younger than myself. Perhaps none of my early playmates are more vividly remembered than is this little maiden.

The name given her by a noted medicine-man was Makah-oesetopah-win. It means The-four-corners-of-the-earth. As she was rather small, the abbreviation with a diminutive termination was considered more appropriate, hence Oesedah became her common name.

Although she had a very good mother, Uncheedah was her efficient teacher and chaperon. Such knowledge as my grandmother deemed suitable to a maiden was duly impressed upon her susceptible mind. When I was not in the woods with Chatanna, Oesedah was my companion at home; and when I returned from my play at evening, she would have a hundred questions ready for me to answer. Some of these were questions concerning our every-day life, and others were more difficult problems which had suddenly dawned upon her active little mind. Whatever had occurred to interest her during the day was immediately repeated for my benefit.

There were certain questions upon which Oesedah held me to be authority, and asked with the hope of increasing her little store of knowledge. I have often heard her declare to her girl companions: "I know it is true; Ohiyesa said so!" Uncheedah was partly responsible for this, for when any questions came up which lay within the sphere of man's observation, she would say:

"Ohiyesa ought to know that: he is a man—I am not! You had better ask him."

The truth was that she had herself explained to me many of the subjects under discussion.

I was occasionally referred to little Oesedah in the same manner, and I always accepted her childish elucidations of any matter upon which I had been advised to consult her, because I knew the source of her wisdom. In this simple way we were made to be teachers of one another.

One day Uncheedah asked her grandchildren, Ohiyesa and Oesedah, a question about what class of animal a lizard was. Ohiyesa said that it belonged to the class of four-legged animals. Oesedah said that it belonged to the class of creeping animals.

The Indians divided all animals into four general classes: 1st, those that walk upon four legs; 2nd, those that fly; 3rd, those that swim with fins; 4th, those that creep.

Of course I endeavored to support my assertion that the lizard belongs where I had placed it, because he has four distinct legs which propel him everywhere, on the ground or in the water. But my opponent claimed that the creature under dispute does not walk, but creeps. My strongest argument was that it had legs; but Oesedah insisted that its body touches the ground as it moves. As a last resort, I volunteered to go find one, and demonstrate the point in question.

The lizard having been brought, we smoothed off the ground and strewed ashes on it so that we could see the track. Then I raised the question: "What constitutes creeping, and what constitutes walking?"

Uncheedah was the judge, and she stated, without any hesitation, that an animal must stand clear of the ground on the support of its legs, and walk with the body above the legs, and not in contact with the ground, in order to be termed a walker; while a creeper is one that, regardless of its legs, if it has them, drags its body upon the ground. Upon hearing the judge's decision, I yielded at once to my opponent.

At another time, when I was engaged in a similar discussion with my brother Chatanna, Oesedah came to my rescue. Our grandmother had asked us:

"What bird shows most judgment in caring for its young?"

Chatanna at once exclaimed:

"The eagle!" but I held my peace for a moment, because I was confused—so many birds came into my mind at once. I finally declared:

"It is the oriole!"

Chatanna was asked to state all the evidence that he had in support of the eagle's good sense in rearing its young. He proceeded with an air of confidence:

"The eagle is the wisest of all birds. Its nest is made in the safest possible place, upon a high and inaccessible cliff. It provides its young with an abundance of fresh meat. They have the freshest of air. They are brought up under the spell of the grandest scenes, and inspired with lofty feelings and bravery.

Ohiyesa's brother Chatanna said that eagles see that all other beings live beneath them. He said that young eaglets are hardy because they are exposed to the weather.

"Why, the little eagles cannot help being as noble as they are, because their parents selected for them so lofty and inspiring a home! How happy they must be when they find themselves above the clouds, and behold the zigzag flashes of lightning all about them! It must be nice to taste a piece of fresh meat up in their cool home, in the burning summer-time! Then when they drop down the bones of the game they feed upon, wolves and vultures gather beneath them, feeding upon their refuse. That alone would show them their chieftainship over all the other birds. Isn't that so, grandmother?" Thus triumphantly he concluded his argument.

I was staggered at first by the noble speech of Chatannna, but I soon recovered from its effects. The little Oesedah came to my aid by saying: "Wait until Ohiyesa tells of the loveliness of the beautiful oriole's home!" This timely remark gave me courage and I began:

"My grandmother, who was it said that a mother who has a gentle and sweet voice will have children of a good disposition? I think the oriole is that kind of a parent. It provides both sunshine and shadow for its young. Its nest is suspended from the prettiest bough of the most graceful tree, where it is rocked by the gentle winds; and the one we found yesterday was beautifully lined with soft things, both deep and warm, so that the little featherless birdies cannot suffer from the cold and wet."

Here Chatanna interrupted me to exclaim: "That is just like the white people—who cares for them? The eagle teaches its young to be accustomed to hardships, like young warriors!"

Ohiyesa was provoked; he reproached his brother and appealed to the judge, saying that he had not finished yet.

"But you would not have lived, Chatanna, if you had been exposed like that when you were a baby! The oriole shows wisdom in providing for its children a good, comfortable home! A home upon a high rock would not be pleasant—it would be cold! We climbed a mountain once, and it was cold there; and who would care to stay in such a place when it storms? What wisdom is there in having a pile of rough sticks upon a bare rock, surrounded with ill-smelling bones of animals, for a home? Also, my uncle says that the eaglets seem always to be on the point of starvation. You have heard that whoever lives on game killed by some one else is compared to an eagle. Isn't that so, grandmother?

"The oriole suspends its nest from the lower side of a horizontal bough so that no enemy can approach it. It enjoys peace and beauty and safety."

Oesedah was at Ohiyesa's side during the discussion, and occasionally whispered into his ear. Uncheedah decided this time in favor of Ohiyesa.

We were once very short of provisions in the winter time. My uncle, our only means of support, was sick; and besides, we were separated from the rest of the tribe and in a region where there was little game of any kind. Oesedah had a pet squirrel, and as soon as we began to economize our food had given portions of her allowance to her pet.

At last we were reduced very much, and the prospect of obtaining anything soon being gloomy, my grandmother reluctantly suggested that the squirrel should be killed for food. Thereupon my little cousin cried, and said:

"Why cannot we all die alike wanting? The squirrel's life is as dear to him as ours to us," and clung to it. Fortunately, relief came in time to save her pet.

15

SMOKY DAY, THE STORYTELLER

Smoky Day was widely known among us as a preserver of history and legend. He was a living book of the traditions and history of his people. Among his effects were bundles of small sticks, notched and painted. One bundle contained the number of his own years. Another was composed of sticks representing the important events of history, each of which was marked with the number of years since that particular event occurred. For instance, there was the year when so many stars fell from the sky, with the number of years since it happened cut into the wood. Another recorded the appearance of a comet; and from these heavenly wonders the great national catastrophes and victories were reckoned.

But I will try to repeat some of his favorite narratives as I heard them from his own lips. I went to him one day with a piece of tobacco and an eagle-feather; not to buy his MSS., but hoping for the privilege of hearing him tell of some of the brave deeds of our people in remote times.

His "MSS" probably means his stories.

The tall and large old man greeted me with his usual courtesy and thanked me for my present. As I recall the meeting, I well remember his unusual stature, his slow speech and gracious manner.

"Ah, Ohiyesa!" said he, "my young warrior—for such you will be some day! I know this by your seeking to hear of the great deeds of your ancestors. That is a good sign, and I love to repeat these stories to one who is destined to be a brave man. I do not wish to lull you to sleep with sweet words; but I know the conduct of your paternal ancestors. They have been and are still among the bravest of our tribe. To prove this, I will relate what happened in your paternal grandfather's family, twenty years ago.

Two of Ohiyesa's great uncles had died at the hands of a member of their own band. Other men in the band wanted to kill the man who had done this terrible deed. Ohiyesa's grandfather said that he and his other brothers would not condescend to spill the blood of someone who had acted so terribly. Smoky Day said:

"These men were foremost among the warriors of the Sioux, and no one questioned their courage; yet when this calamity was brought upon them by a villain, they refused to touch him! This, my boy, is a test of true bravery. Self-possession and self-control at such a moment is proof of a strong heart.

"You have heard of Jingling Thunder the elder, whose brave deeds are well known to the Villagers of the Lakes.

Smoky Day began his story about Jingling Thunder:

"Many winters ago there was a great battle, in which Jingling Thunder won his first honors. It was forty winters before the falling of many stars, which event occurred twenty winters after the coming of the black-robed white priest; and that was fourteen winters before the annihilation by our people of thirty lodges of the Sac and Fox Indians. I well remember the latter event—it was just fifty winters ago. However, I will count my sticks again."

So saying, Smoky Day produced his bundle of

variously colored sticks, about five inches long. He counted and gave them to me to verify his calculation.

"But you," he resumed, "do not care to remember the winters that have passed. You are young, and care only for the event and the deed. It was very many years ago that this thing happened that I am about to tell you, and yet our people speak of it with as much enthusiasm as if it were only yesterday. Our heroes are always kept alive in the minds of the nation.

"Our people lived then on the east bank of the Mississippi, a little south of where Imnejah-skah, or White Cliff (St. Paul, Minnesota), now stands. After they left Mille Lacs they founded several villages, but finally settled in this spot, whence the tribes have gradually dispersed. Here a battle occurred which surpassed all others in history. It lasted one whole day—the Sacs and Foxes and the Dakotas against the Ojibways.

Smoky Day described the battle to Ohiyesa.

That night I lay awake a long time committing to memory the tradition I had heard, and the next day I boasted to my playmate, Little Rainbow, about my first lesson from the old storyteller. To this he replied:

"I would rather have Weyuhah for my teacher. I think he remembers more than any of the others. When Weyuhah tells about a battle you can see it yourself; you can even hear the war-whoop," he went on with much enthusiasm.

"That is what his friends say of him; but those who are not his friends say that he brings many warriors into the battle who were not there," I answered indignantly, for I could not admit that old Smoky Day could have a rival.

Before I went to him again Uncheedah had thoughtfully prepared a nice venison roast for the teacher, and I was proud to take him something good to eat before beginning his story.

"How," was his greeting, "so you have begun already, Ohiyesa? Your family were ever feastmakers as well as warriors."

16

THE MAIDENS' FEAST

There were many peculiar customs among the Indians of an earlier period, some of which tended to strengthen the character of the people and preserve their purity. Perhaps the most unique of these was the annual "feast of maidens." The casual observer would scarcely understand the full force and meaning of this ceremony.

The last one that I ever witnessed was given at Fort Ellis, Manitoba, about the year 1871. Upon the table land just back of the old trading post and fully a thousand feet above the Assiniboine river, surrounded by groves, there was a natural amphitheater. At one end stood the old fort where since 1830 the northern tribes had come to replenish their powder horns and lead sacks and to dispose of their pelts.

In this spot there was a reunion of all the renegade Sioux on the one hand and of the Assiniboines and

Crees, the Canadian tribes, on the other. They were friendly. The matter was not formally arranged, but it was usual for all the tribes to meet here in the month of July.

The Hudson Bay Company always had a good supply of red, blue, green and white blankets, also cloth of brilliant dye, so that when their summer festival occurred the Indians did not lack gayly colored garments. Paints were bought by them at pleasure. Short sleeves were the fashion in their buckskin dresses, and beads and porcupine quills were the principal decorations.

When circumstances are favorable, the Indians are the happiest people in the world. There were entertainments every single day, which everybody had the fullest opportunity to see and enjoy. If anything, the poorest profited the most by these occasions, because a feature in each case was the giving away of savage wealth to the needy in honor of the event. At any public affair, involving the pride and honor of a prominent family, there must always be a distribution of valuable presents.

One bright summer morning, while we were still at our meal of jerked buffalo meat, we heard the herald of the Wahpeton band upon his calico pony as he rode around our circle.

"White Eagle's daughter, the maiden Red Star,

invites all the maidens of all the tribes to come and partake of her feast. It will be in the Wahpeton camp, before the sun reaches the middle of the sky. All pure maidens are invited. Red Star also invites the young men to be present, to see that no unworthy maiden should join in the feast."

The herald soon completed the rounds of the different camps, and it was not long before the girls began to gather in great numbers. The fort was fully alive to the interest of these savage entertainments.

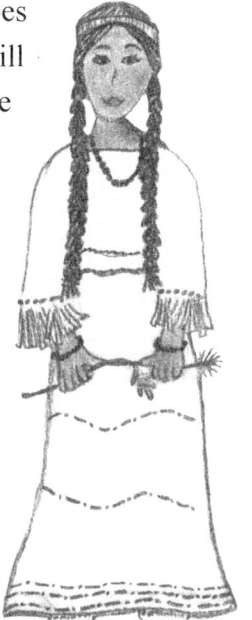

The Maidens' Feast was a solemn ceremony. The maidens, the young men, and the older people took it very seriously.

The youths had a similar feast of their own, in which the eligibles were those who had never spoken to a girl in the way of courtship. It was considered ridiculous so to do before attaining some honor as a warrior, and the novices prided themselves greatly upon their self control.

From the various camps the girls came singly or in groups, dressed in bright-colored calicoes or in heavily fringed and beaded buckskin. Their smooth cheeks and the central part of their glossy hair was touched with vermilion. All brought with them wooden basins to eat from. Some who came from a considerable distance were mounted upon ponies; a few, for company or novelty's sake, rode double.

The maidens' circle was formed about a coneshaped rock which stood upon its base. This was painted red. Beside it two new arrows were lightly stuck into the ground.

Each maiden lightly touched the rock and the arrows, which was her way of promising that she was pure.

Immediately behind the maidens' circle is the old women's or chaperons' circle. This second circle is almost as interesting to look at as the inner one. The old women watched every movement of their respective charges with the utmost concern, having previously instructed them how they should conduct themselves in any event.

There was never a more gorgeous assembly of the kind than this one. The day was perfect. The Crees, displaying their characteristic horsemanship, came in groups; the Assiniboines, with their curious pompadour well covered with red paint. The various bands of Sioux all carefully observed the traditional peculiarities of dress and behavior. The attaches of the fort were fully represented at the entertainment, and it was not unusual to see a pale-face maiden take part in the feast.

The maidens sang their maidens' song and danced around the rock four times.

Each maid as she departed once more took her oath to remain pure until she should meet her husband.

17

THE FALL HUNT

The month of September recalls to every Indian's mind the season of the fall hunt. I remember one such expedition which is typical of many. Our party appeared on the northwestern side of Turtle Mountain; for we had been hunting buffaloes all summer, in the region of the Mouse River, between that mountain and the upper Missouri.

As our cone-shaped teepees rose in clusters along the outskirts of the heavy forest that clothes the sloping side of the mountain, the scene below was gratifying to a savage eye. The rolling yellow plains were checkered with herds of buffaloes. Along the banks of the streams that ran down from the mountains were also many elk, which usually appear at morning and evening, and disappear into the forest during the warmer part of the day. Deer, too, were plenty, and the brooks were alive with trout. Here and there the streams were dammed by the industrious beaver.

In the interior of the forest there were lakes with many islands, where moose, elk, deer and bears were abundant. The water-fowl were wont to gather here in great numbers, among them the crane, the swan, the loon, and many of the smaller kinds. The forest also was filled with a great variety of birds. Here the partridge drummed his loudest, while the whippoorwill sang with spirit, and the hooting owl reigned in the night.

To me, as a boy, this wilderness was a paradise. It was a land of plenty. To be sure, we did not have any of the luxuries of civilization, but we had every convenience and opportunity and luxury of Nature. We had also the gift of enjoying our good fortune, whatever dangers might lurk about us; and the truth is that we lived in blessed ignorance of any life that was better than our own.

As soon as hunting in the woods began, the customs regulating it were established. The council teepee no longer existed. A hunting bonfire was kindled every morning at day-break, at which each brave must appear and report. The man who failed to do this before the party set out on the day's hunt was harassed by ridicule. As a rule, the hunters started before sunrise, and the brave who was announced throughout the camp as the first one to return with a deer on his back, was a man to be envied.

The legend-teller, old Smoky Day, was chosen herald of the camp, and it was he who made the announcements. After supper was ended, we heard his powerful voice resound among the teepees in the forest. He would then name a man to kindle the bonfire the next morning. His suit of fringed buckskin set off his splendid physique to advantage.

Scarcely had the men disappeared in the woods each morning than all the boys sallied forth, apparently engrossed in their games and sports, but in reality competing actively with one another in quickness of observation. As the day advanced, they all kept the sharpest possible lookout. Suddenly there would come the shrill "Woo-coohoo!" at the top of a boy's voice, announcing the bringing in of a deer. Immediately all the other boys took up the cry, each one bent on getting ahead of the rest. Now we all saw the brave Wacoota fairly bent over by his burden, a large deer which he carried on his shoulders. His fringed buckskin shirt was besprinkled with blood. He threw down the deer at the door of his wife's mother's home, according to custom, and then walked proudly to his own. At the door of his father's teepee he stood for a moment straight as a pine-tree, and then entered.

When a bear was brought in, a hundred or more of these urchins were wont to make the woods resound with their voices: "Wah! wah! wah! Wah! wah! wah! The brave White Rabbit brings a bear! Wah! wah! wah!"

All day these sing-song cheers were kept up, as the game was brought in. At last, toward the close of the afternoon, all the hunters had returned, and happiness and contentment reigned absolute, in a fashion which I have never observed among the white people, even in the best of circumstances. The men were lounging and smoking; the women actively engaged in the preparation of the evening meal, and the care of the meat.

During this September, the hunting went well. Meat was so abundant that the men stopped hunting deer, elk, and moose for a while.

Only the hunting for pelts, such as those of the bear, beaver, marten, and otter was continued. But whenever we lived in blessed abundance, our braves were wont to turn their thoughts to other occupations—especially the hot-blooded youths whose ambition it was to do something noteworthy.

The young men got restless and wanted to fight people of the Gros Ventre nation.

On the appointed morning we heard the songs of the warriors and the wailing of the women, by which they bade adieu to each other, and the eligible braves, headed by an experienced man—old Hotanka or Loud-Voiced Raven—set out for the Gros Ventre country.

Our older heads, to be sure, had expressed some disapproval of the undertaking, for the country in which we were roaming was not our own, and we were likely at any time to be taken to task by its rightful owners. The plain truth of the matter was that we were intruders. Hence the more thoughtful among us preferred to be at home, and to achieve what renown they could get by defending their homes and families. The young men, however, were so eager for action and excitement that they must needs go off in search of it.

From the early morning when these braves left us, led by the old war-priest, Loud-Voiced Raven, the anxious mothers, sisters and sweethearts counted the days.

Old Smoky Day would occasionally get up early in the morning, and sing a "strong-heart" song for his absent grandson. I still seem to hear the hoarse, cracked voice of the ancient singer as it resounded among the woods. For a long time our roving community enjoyed unbroken peace, and we were spared any trouble or disturbance. Our hunters often brought in a deer or elk or bear for fresh meat. The beautiful lakes furnished us with fish and wild-fowl for variety. Their placid waters, as the autumn advanced, reflected the variegated colors of the changing foliage.

It is my recollection that we were at this time encamped in the vicinity of the "Turtle Mountain's Heart." It is to the highest cone-shaped peak that the Indians aptly give this appellation. Our camping-ground for two months was within a short distance of the peak, and the men made it a point to often send one of their number to the top. It was understood between them and the war party that we were to remain near this spot; and on their return trip the latter were to give the "smoke sign," which we would answer from the top of the hill.

Ohiyesa's band continued to enjoy the fall. The young warriors had still not returned.

The leaves had now begun to fall, and the heavy frosts made the nights very cold. We were forced to realize that the short summer of that region had said adieu! Still we were gay and lighthearted, for we had plenty of provisions, and no misfortune had yet overtaken us in our wanderings over the country for nearly three months.

One day old Smoky Day returned from the daily hunt with an alarm. He had seen a sign—a "smoke sign." This had not appeared in the quarter that they were anxiously watching—it came from the east. After a long consultation among the men, it was concluded from the nature and duration of the smoke that it proceeded from an accidental fire. It was further surmised that the fire was not made by Sioux, since it was out of their country, but by a war-party of Ojibways, who were accustomed to use matches when lighting their pipes, and to throw them carelessly away. It was thought that a little time had been spent in an attempt to put it out.

The council decreed that a strict look-out should be established in behalf of our party. Every day a scout was appointed to reconnoitre in the direction of the smoke. It was agreed that no gun should be fired for twelve days. All our signals were freshly rehearsed among the men. The women and old men went so far as to dig little convenient holes around their lodges, for defense in case of a sudden attack. And yet an Ojibway scout would not have suspected, from the ordinary appearance of the camp, that the Sioux had become aware of their neighborhood! Scouts were stationed just outside of the village at night. They had been so trained as to rival an owl or a cat in their ability to see in the dark.

The twelve days passed by, however, without bringing any evidence of the nearness of the supposed

Ojibway war-party, and the "lookout" established for purposes of protection was abandoned. Soon after this, one morning at dawn, we were aroused by the sound of the unwelcome warwhoop. Although only a child, I sprang up and was about to rush out, as I had been taught to do; but my good grandmother pulled me down, and gave me a sign to lay flat on the ground. I sharpened my ears and lay still.

All was quiet in camp, but at some little distance from us there was a lively encounter. I could distinctly hear the old herald, shouting and yelling in exasperation. "Whoo! whoo!" was the signal of distress, and I could almost hear the pulse of my own blood-vessels.

Closer and closer the struggle came, and still the women appeared to grow more and more calm.

This was indeed an Ojibwe attack. The Sioux charged them and they ran away, but Smoky Day and another man, White Crane, died during the fight. One day one of the warriors who had gone away to fight came back alone. All of the other young men who had gone to fight died in their battle against the Gros Ventre.

18

WINTER CAMP

When I was about twelve years old we wintered upon the Mouse River, west of Turtle Mountain. It was one of the coldest winters I ever knew, and was so regarded by the old men of the tribe. The summer before there had been plenty of buffalo upon that side of the Missouri, and our people had made many packs of dried buffalo meat and cached them in different places, so that they could get them in case of need. There were many black-tailed deer and elk along the river, and grizzlies were to be found in the open country. Apparently there was no danger of starvation, so our people thought to winter there; but it proved to be a hard winter.

There was a great snow-fall, and the cold was intense. The snow was too deep for hunting, and the main body of the buffalo had crossed the Missouri, where it was too far to go after them. But there were some smaller herds of the animals scattered about in our vicinity, therefore there was still fresh meat to be had, but it was not secured without a great deal of difficulty.

No ponies could be used. The men hunted on snowshoes until after the Moon of Sore Eyes (March), when after a heavy thaw a crust was formed on the snow which would scarcely hold a man. It was then that our people hunted buffalo with dogs—an unusual expedient.

Sleds were made of buffalo ribs and hickory saplings, the runners bound with rawhide with the hair side down. These slipped smoothly over the icy crust. Only small men rode on the sleds. When buffalo were reported by the hunting-scouts, everybody had his dog team ready. All went under orders from the police, and approached the herd under cover until they came within charging distance.

The men had their bows and arrows, and a few had guns. The huge animals could not run fast in the deep snow. They all followed a leader, trampling out a narrow path. The dogs with their drivers soon caught up with them on each side, and the hunters brought many of them down.

I remember when the party returned, late in the night. The men came in single file, well loaded, and each dog following his master with an equally heavy load. Both men and animals were white with frost.

We boys had waited impatiently for their arrival. As soon as we spied them coming a buffalo hunting whistle was started, and every urchin in the village added his voice to the weird sound, while the dogs who had been left at home joined with us in the chorus. The men, wearing their buffalo moccasins with the hair inside and robes of the same, came home hungry and exhausted.

It is often supposed that the dog in the Indian camp is a useless member of society, but it is not so in the wild life. We found him one of the most useful of domestic animals, especially in an emergency.

A little way from our camp there was a log village of French Canadian half-breeds, but the two villages did not intermingle. About the Moon of Difficulty (January) we were initiated into some of the peculiar customs of our neighbors. In the middle of the night there was a firing of guns throughout their village. Some of the people thought they had been attacked, and went over to assist them, but to their surprise they were told that this was the celebration of the birth of the new year!

The next day the people who were half-French Canadian and half-Native American invited Ohiyesa's village to a dance.

I never knew before that a new year begins in midwinter. We had always counted that the year ends when the winter ends, and a new year begins with the new life in the springtime.

I was now taken for the first time to a white man's dance in a log house. I thought it was the dizziest thing I ever saw. One man sat in a corner, sawing away at a stringed board, and all the while he was stamping the floor with his foot and giving an occasional shout. When he called out, the dancers seemed to move faster.

The men danced with women—something that we Indians never do—and when the man in the corner shouted they would swing the women around. It looked very rude to me, as I stood outside with the other boys and peeped through the chinks in the logs. At one time a young man and woman facing each other danced in the middle of the floor. I thought they would surely wear their moccasins out against the rough boards; but after a few minutes they were relieved by another couple.

Then an old man with long curly hair and a fox-skin cap danced alone in the middle of the room, slapping the floor with his moccasined foot in a lightning fashion that I have never seen equalled. He seemed to be a leader among them.

19

HAPPY HARVEST DAYS

When our people lived in Minnesota, a good part of their natural subsistence was furnished by the wild rice, which grew abundantly in all of that region. Around the shores and all over some of the innumerable lakes of the "Land of Sky-blue Water" was this wild cereal found. Indeed, some of the watery fields in those days might be compared in extent and fruitfulness with the fields of wheat on Minnesota's magnificent farms to-day.

The wild rice harvesters came in groups of fifteen to twenty families to a lake, depending upon the size of the harvest. Some of the Indians hunted buffalo upon the prairie at this season, but there were more who preferred to go to the lakes to gather wild rice, fish, gather berries and hunt the deer. There was an abundance of water-fowls among the grain; and really no season of the year was happier than this.

The camping-ground was usually an attractive spot, with shade and cool breezes off the water. The people, while they pitched their teepees upon the heights, if possible, for the sake of a good outlook, actually lived in their canoes upon the placid waters. The happiest of all, perhaps, were the young maidens, who were all day long in their canoes, in twos or threes, and when tired of gathering the wild cereal, would sit in the boats doing their needle-work.

These maidens learned to imitate the calls of the different water-fowls as a sort of signal to the members of a group. Even the old women and the boys adopted signals, so that while the population of the village was lost to sight in a thick field of wild rice, a meeting could be arranged without calling any one by his or her own name. It was a great convenience for those young men who sought opportunity to meet certain maidens, for there were many canoe paths through the rice.

August is the harvest month.

Ohiyesa's band prepared for the harvesting of wild rice.

Women and men were making birch canoes, for nearly every member of the family must be provided with one for this occasion. The blueberry and huckleberry-picking also preceded the rice-gathering.

There were social events which enlivened the camp of the harvesters; such as maidens' feasts, dances and a canoe regatta or two, in which not only the men were participants, but women and young girls as well.

On the appointed day all the canoes were carried to the shore and placed upon the water.

Each family had worked in their own allotted field. They tied rice into bundles and let it stand for a few days.

Then they again entered the lake, assigning two persons to each canoe. One manipulated the paddle, while the foremost one gently drew the heads of each bundle toward him and gave it a few strokes with a light rod. This caused the rice to fall into the bottom of the craft. The field was traversed in this manner back and forth until finished.

This was the pleasantest and easiest part of the

harvest toil. The real work was when they prepared the rice for use. First of all, it must be made perfectly dry. They would spread it upon buffalo robes and mats, and sometimes upon layers of coarse swamp grass, and dry it in the sun. If the time was short, they would make a scaffold and spread upon it a certain thickness of the green grass and afterward the rice. Under this a fire was made, taking care that the grass did not catch fire.

When all the rice is gathered and dried, the hulling begins. A round hole is dug about two feet deep and the same in diameter. Then the rice is heated over a fireplace, and emptied into the hole while it is hot. A young man, having washed his feet and put on a new pair of moccasins, treads upon it until all is hulled. The women then pour it upon a robe and begin to shake it so that the chaff will be separated by the wind. Some of the rice is browned before being hulled.

During the hulling time there were prizes offered to the young men who can hull quickest and best. There were sometimes from twenty to fifty youths dancing with their feet in these holes.

Pretty moccasins were brought by shy maidens to the youths of their choice, asking them to hull rice. There were daily entertainments which deserved some such name as "hulling bee"—at any rate, we all enjoyed them hugely. The girls brought with them plenty of good things to eat.

When all the rice was prepared for the table, the matter of storing it must be determined. Caches were dug by each family in a concealed spot, and carefully lined with dry grass and bark. Here they left their surplus stores for a time of need. Our people were very ingenious in covering up all traces of the hidden food. A common trick was to build a fire on top of the mound. As much of the rice as could be carried conveniently was packed in par-fleches, or cases made of rawhide, and brought back with us to our village.

After all, the wild Indians could not be justly termed improvident, when their manner of life is taken into consideration. They let nothing go to waste, and labored incessantly during the summer and fall to lay up provision for the inclement season. Berries of all kinds were industriously gathered, and dried in the sun. Even the wild cherries were pounded up, stones and all, made into small cakes and dried for use in soups and for mixing with the pounded jerked meat and fat to form a much-prized Indian delicacy.

Out on the prairie in July and August the women were wont to dig teepsinna with sharpened sticks, and many a bag full was dried and put away. This teepsinna is the root of a certain plant growing mostly upon high sandy soil. It is starchy but solid, with a sweetish taste, and is very fattening. The fully grown teepsinna is two or three inches long, and has a dark-brown bark not unlike the bark of a young tree. It can be eaten raw or stewed, and is always kept in a dried state, except when it is first dug.

There was another root that our people gathered in small quantities. It is a wild sweet potato, found in bottom lands or river beds.

The primitive housekeeper exerted herself much to secure a variety of appetizing dishes; she even robbed the field mouse and the muskrat to accomplish her end. The tiny mouse gathers for her winter use several excellent kinds of food. Among these is a wild bean which equals in flavor any domestic bean that I have ever tasted. Her storehouse is usually under a peculiar mound, which the untrained eye would be unable to distinguish from an ant-hill. There are many pockets underneath, into which she industriously gathers the harvest of the summer.

She is fortunate if the quick eye of a native woman does not detect her hiding-place. About the month of September, while traveling over the prairie, a woman is occasionally observed to halt suddenly and waltz around a suspected mound. Finally the pressure of her heel causes a place to give way, and she settles contentedly down to rob the poor mouse of the fruits of her labor.

The different kinds of beans are put away in different pockets, but it is the oomenechah she wants. The field mouse loves this savory vegetable, for she always gathers it more than any other. There is also some of the white star-like manakcahkcah, the root of the wild lily. This is a good medicine and good to eat.

When our people were gathering the wild rice, they always watched for another plant that grows in the muddy bottom of lakes and ponds. It is a white bulb about the size of an ordinary onion. This is stored away by the muskrats in their houses by the waterside, and there is often a bushel or more of the psinchinchah to be found within.

20

A MEETING ON THE PLAINS

We were encamped at one time on the Souris or Mouse River, a tributary of the Assiniboine. The buffaloes were still plenty; hence we were living on the "fat of the land." One afternoon a scout came in with the announcement that a body of United States troops was approaching! This report, of course, caused much uneasiness among our people.

A council was held immediately, in the course of which the scout was put through a rigid examination. Before a decision had been reached, another scout came in from the field. He declared that the moving train reported as a body of troops was in reality a train of Canadian carts.

The two reports differed so widely that it was deemed wise to send out more runners to observe this moving body closely, and ascertain definitely its character.

These soon returned with the positive information that the Canadians were at hand, "for," said they, "there are no bright metals in the moving train to send forth flashes of light. The separate bodies are short, like carts with ponies, and not like the long, four-wheeled wagon drawn by four or six mules, that the soldiers use. They are not buffaloes, and they cannot be mounted troops, with pack-mules, because the individual bodies are too long for that. Besides, the soldiers usually have their chief, with his guards, leading the train; and the little chiefs are also separated from the main body and ride at one side!"

From these observations it was concluded that we were soon to meet with the bois brules, as the French call their mixed-bloods, presumably from the color of their complexions. Some say that they are named from the "burned forests" which, as wood-cutters, they are accustomed to leave behind them. Two or three hours later, at about sunset, our ears began to distinguish the peculiar music that always accompanied a moving train of their carts. It is like the grunting and squealing of many animals, and is due to the fact that the wheels and all other parts of these vehicles are made of wood. Our dogs gleefully augmented the volume of inharmonious sound.

They stopped a little way from our camp, upon a grassy plain, and the ponies were made to wheel their clumsy burdens into a perfect circle, the shafts being turned inward. Thus was formed a sort of barricade—quite a usual and necessary precaution in their nomadic and adventurous life. Within this circle the tents were pitched, and many cheerful fires were soon kindled. The garcons were hurriedly driving the ponies to water, with much cracking of whips and outbursting of impatient oaths.

Our chief and his principal warriors briefly conferred with the strangers, and it was understood by both parties that no thought of hostilities lurked in the minds of either.

After having observed the exchange of presents that always follows a "peace council," there were friendly and hospitable feasts in both camps.

Ohiyesa's people got a surprise in the middle of the night.

Suddenly the loud report of a gun stirred the sleepers. Many more reports were heard in quick succession, all coming from the camp of the bois brules. Every man among the Sioux sprang to his feet, weapon in hand, and many ran towards their ponies. But there was one significant point about the untimely firing of the guns—they were all directed heavenward! One of our old men, who understood better than any one else the manners of the half-breeds, thus proclaimed at the top of his voice:

"Let the people sleep! This that we have heard is the announcement of a boy's advent into the world! It is their custom to introduce with gunpowder a new-born boy!"

21

THE FUNNY PHILOSOPHER

There is scarcely anything so exasperating to me as the idea that the natives of this country have no sense of humor and no faculty for mirth. This phase of their character is well understood by those whose fortune or misfortune it has been to live among them day in and day out at their homes. I don't believe I ever heard a real hearty laugh away from the Indians' fireside. I have often spent an entire evening in laughing with them until I could laugh no more. There are evenings when the recognized wit or story-teller of the village gives a free entertainment which keeps the rest of the community in a convulsive state until he leaves them. However, Indian humor consists as much in the gestures and inflections of the voice as in words, and is really untranslatable.

Matogee (Yellow Bear) was a natural humorous speaker, and a very diffident man at other times. He usually said little, but when he was in the mood he could keep a large company in a roar. This was especially the case whenever he met his brother-in-law, Tamedokah.

It was a custom with us Indians to joke more particularly with our brothers- and sisters-in-law. But no one ever complained, or resented any of these jokes, however personal they might be. That would be an unpardonable breach of etiquette.

"Tamedokah, I heard that you tried to capture a buck by holding on to his tail," said Matogee, laughing. "I believe that feat cannot be performed any more; at least, it never has been since the pale-face brought us the knife, the 'mysterious iron,' and the pulverized coal that makes bullets fly. Since our ancestors hunted with stone knives and hatchets, I say, that has never been done."

The fact was that Tamedokah had stunned a buck that day while hunting, and as he was about to dress him the animal got up and attempted to run, whereupon the Indian launched forth to secure his game. He only succeeded in grasping the tail of the deer, and was pulled about all over the meadows and the adjacent woods until the tail came off in his hands. Matogee thought this too good a joke to be lost.

I sat near the door of the tent, and thoroughly enjoyed the story of the comical accident.

"Yes," Tamedokah quietly replied, "I thought I

would do something to beat the story of the man who rode a young elk, and yelled frantically for help, crying like a woman."

"Ugh! that was only a legend," retorted Matogee, for it was he who was the hero of this tale in his younger days. "But this is a fresh feat of to-day. Chankpayuhah said he could not tell which was the most scared, the buck or you," he continued. "He said the deer's eyes were bulging out of their sockets, while Tamedokah's mouth was constantly enlarging toward his ears, and his hair floated on the wind, shaking among the branches of the trees. That will go down with the traditions of our fathers," he concluded with an air of satisfaction.

"It was a singular mishap," admitted Tamedokah.

The pipe had been filled by Matogee and passed to Tamedokah good-naturedly, still with a broad smile on his face. "It must be acknowledged," he resumed, "that you have the strongest kind of a grip, for no one else could hold on as long as you did, and secure such a trophy besides. That tail will do for an eagle feather holder."

By this time the teepee was packed to overflowing. Loud laughter had been heard issuing from the lodge of Matogee, and everybody suspected that he had something good, so many had come to listen.

"I think we should hear the whole matter," said one of the late comers.

The teepee was brightly lit by the burning embers, and all the men were sitting with their knees up against their chests, held in that position by wrapping their robes tightly around loins and knees. This fixed them something in the fashion of a rocking-chair.

"Well, no one saw him except Chankpayuhah," Matogee remarked.

"Yes, yes, he must tell us about it," exclaimed a chorus of voices.

"This is what I saw," the witness began. "I was tracking a buck and a doe. As I approached a small opening at the creek side 'boom!' came a report of the mysterious iron. I remained in a stooping position, hoping to see a deer cross the opening. In this I was not disappointed, for immediately after the report a fine buck dashed forth with Tamedokah close behind him. The latter was holding on to the deer's tail with both hands and his knife was in his mouth, but it soon dropped out. 'Tamedokah,' I shouted, 'haven't you got hold of the wrong animal?' but as I spoke they disappeared into the woods.

"In a minute they both appeared again, and then it was that I began to laugh. I could not stop. It almost killed me. The deer jumped the longest jumps I ever saw. Tamedokah walked the longest paces and was very swift. His hair was whipping the trees as they went by. Water poured down his face. I stood bent forward because I could not straighten my back-bone, and was ready to fall when they again disappeared.

"When they came out for the third time it seemed as if the woods and the meadow were moving too. Tamedokah skipped across the opening as if he were a grasshopper learning to hop. I fell down.

"When I came to he was putting water on my face and head, but when I looked at him I fell again, and did not know anything until the sun had passed the mid-sky."

The company was kept roaring all the way through this account, while Tamedokah himself heartily joined in the mirth.

"Ho, ho, ho!" they said; "he has made his name famous in our annals. This will be told of him henceforth."

"It reminds me of Chadozee's bear story," said one.

"His was more thrilling, because it was really dangerous," interposed another.

"You can tell it to us, Bobdoo," remarked a third.

The man thus addressed made no immediate reply. He was smoking contentedly. At last he silently returned the pipe to Matogee, with whom it had begun its rounds. Deliberately he tightened his robe around him, saying as he did so:

"Ho (Yes). I was with him. It was by a very little that he saved his life. I will tell you how it happened.

"I was hunting with these two men, Nageedah and Chadozee. We came to some wild cherry bushes. I began to eat of the fruit when I saw a large silver-tip crawling toward us. 'Look out! there is a grizzly here,' I shouted, and I ran my pony out on to the prairie; but the others had already dismounted.

"Nageedah had just time to jump upon his pony and get out of the way, but the bear seized hold of his robe and pulled it off. Chadozee stood upon the verge of a steep bank, below which there ran a deep and swift-flowing stream. The bear rushed upon him so suddenly that when he took a step backward, they both fell into the creek together. It was a fall of about twice the height of a man."

"Did they go out of sight?" someone inquired.

"Yes, both fell headlong. In his excitement Chadozee laid hold of the bear in the water, and I never saw a bear try so hard to get away from a man as this one did."

"Ha, ha, ha! ha, ha, ha!" they all laughed.

"When they came to the surface again they were both so eager to get to the shore that each let go, and they swam as quickly as they could to opposite sides. Chadozee could not get any further, so he clung to a stray root, still keeping a close watch of the bear, who was forced to do the same. There they both hung, regarding each other with looks of contempt and defiance."

22

FIRST IMPRESSIONS OF THE WHITE MAN'S WORLD

I have already told how I was adopted into the family of my father's younger brother, when my father was betrayed and imprisoned.

Ohiyesa and his family believed that his father and brothers had been executed. Ohiyesa's uncle had taught him that he must avenge the death of his father and brothers.

Now the savage philosophers looked upon vengeance in the field of battle as a lofty virtue. To avenge the death of a relative or of a dear friend was considered a great deed. My uncle, accordingly, had spared no pains to instill into my young mind the obligation to avenge the death of my father and my older brothers. Already I looked eagerly forward to the day when I should find an opportunity to carry out his teachings.

Ohiyesa hated white men—whom he also called Big Knives or Washechu—but he was curious about the stories he had heard about them.

On the other hand, I had heard marvelous things of this people. In some things we despised them; in others we regarded them as wakan (mysterious), a race whose power bordered upon the supernatural. I learned that they had made a "fireboat." I could not understand how they could unite two elements which cannot exist together. I thought the water would put out the fire, and the fire would consume the boat if it had the shadow of a chance. This was to me a preposterous thing! But when I was told that the Big Knives had created a "fire-boat-walks-on-mountains" (a locomotive) it was too much to believe.

"Why," declared my informant, "those who saw this monster move said that it flew from mountain to mountain when it seemed to be excited. They said also that they believed it carried a thunder-bird, for they frequently heard his usual war-whoop as the creature sped along!"

Several warriors had observed from a distance one of the first trains on the Northern Pacific, and had gained an exaggerated impression of the wonders of the paleface. They had seen it go over a bridge that spanned a deep ravine and it seemed to them that it jumped from one bank to the other. I confess that the story almost quenched my ardor and bravery.

Two or three young men were talking together about this fearful invention.

"However," said one, "I understand that this fire-boat-walks-on-mountains cannot move except on the track made for it."

Although a boy is not expected to join in the conversation of his elders, I ventured to ask: "Then it cannot chase us into any rough country?"

"No, it cannot do that," was the reply, which I heard with a great deal of relief.

I had seen guns and various other things brought to us by the French Canadians, so that I had already some notion of the supernatural gifts of the white man; but I had never before heard such tales as I listened to that morning. It was said that they had bridged the Missouri and Mississippi Rivers, and that they made immense houses of stone and brick, piled on top of one another until they were as high as high hills. My brain was puzzled with these things for many a day.

The Santee Sioux believed in a power they called the Great Mystery.

Finally I asked my uncle why the Great Mystery gave such power to the Washechu (the rich)—sometimes we called them by this name—and not to us Dakotas.

"For the same reason," he answered, "that he gave to Duta [Red] the skill to make fine bows and arrows, and to Wachesne no skill to make anything."

"And why do the Big Knives increase so much more in number than the Dakotas?" I continued.

"It has been said, and I think it must be true, that they have larger families than we do. I went into the house of an Eashecha (a German), and I counted no less than nine children. The eldest of them could not have been over fifteen. When my grandfather first visited them, down at the mouth of the Mississippi, they were comparatively few; later my father visited their Great Father at Washington, and they had already spread over the whole country."

Ohiyesa's uncle condemned the American practice of slavery.

"Certainly they are a heartless nation. They have made some of their people servants—yes, slaves! We have never believed in keeping slaves, but it seems that these Washechu do!

"The greatest object of their lives seems to be to acquire possessions—to be rich. They desire to possess the whole world. For thirty years they were trying to entice us to sell them our land. Finally the outbreak gave them all, and we have been driven away from our beautiful country.

The "outbreak" Ohiyesa mentions here is the Civil War.

"They are a wonderful people. They have divided the day into hours, like the moons of the year. In fact, they measure everything. Not one of them would let so much as a turnip go from his field unless he received full value for it. I understand that their great men make a feast and invite many, but when the feast is over the guests are required to pay for what they have eaten before leaving the house. I myself saw at White Cliff (the name given to St. Paul, Minnesota) a man who kept a brass drum and a bell to call people to his table; but when he got them in he would make them pay for the food!

"I am also informed," said my uncle, "but this I hardly believe, that their Great Chief (President) compels every man to pay him for the land he lives upon and all his personal goods—even for his own existence—every year!" (This was his idea of taxation.) "I am sure we could not live under such a law.

"When the outbreak occurred, we thought that our

opportunity had come, for we had learned that the Big Knives were fighting among themselves, on account of a dispute over their slaves. It was said that the Great Chief had allowed slaves in one part of the country and not in another, so there was jealousy, and they had to fight it out. We don't know how true this was.

"There were some praying-men who came to us some time before the trouble arose. They observed every seventh day as a holy day. On that day they met in a house that they had built for that purpose, to sing, pray, and speak of their Great Mystery. I was never in one of these meetings. I understand that they had a large book from which they read. By all accounts they were very different from all other white men we have known, for these never observed any such day, and we never knew them to pray, neither did they ever tell us of their Great Mystery.

"In war they have leaders and war-chiefs of different grades. The common warriors are driven forward like a herd of antelopes to face the foe. It is on account of this manner of fighting—from compulsion and not from personal bravery—that we count no coup on them. A lone warrior can do much harm to a large army of them in a bad country."

It was this talk with my uncle that gave me my first clear idea of the white man.

I was almost fifteen years old when my uncle presented me with a flint-lock gun. The possession of the "mysterious iron," and the explosive dirt, or "pulverized coal," as it is called, filled me with new thoughts. All the war-songs that I had ever heard from childhood came back to me with their heroes. It seemed as if I were an entirely new being—the boy had become a man!

"I am now old enough," said I to myself, "and I must beg my uncle to take me with him on his next war-path. I shall soon be able to go among the whites whenever I wish, and to avenge the blood of my father and my brothers."

Ohiyesa began to think very seriously.

My people saw very little of me during the day, for in solitude I found the strength I needed. I groped about in the wilderness, and determined to assume my position as a man. My boyish ways were departing, and a sullen dignity and composure was taking their place.

The thought of love did not hinder my ambitions. I had a vague dream of some day courting a pretty maiden, after I had made my reputation, and won the eagle feathers.

One day, when I was away on the daily hunt, two strangers from the United States visited our camp. They had boldly ventured across the northern border. They were Indians, but clad in the white man's garments. It was as well that I was absent with my gun.

My father, accompanied by an Indian guide, after many days' searching had found us at last.

Ohiyesa's father had been a prisoner in Davenport, Iowa, with other people who took part in the U.S.-Dakota War of 1862.

He was taught in prison and converted by the pioneer missionaries, Drs. Williamson and Riggs. He was under sentence of death, but was among the number against whom no direct evidence was found, and who were finally pardoned by President Lincoln.

When he was released, and returned to the new reservation upon the Missouri River, he soon became convinced that life on a government reservation meant physical and moral degradation. Therefore he determined, with several others, to try the white man's way of gaining a livelihood. They accordingly left the agency against the persuasions of the agent, renounced all government assistance, and took land under the United States Homestead law, on the Big Sioux river. After he had made his home there, he desired to seek his lost child. It was then a dangerous undertaking to cross the line, but his Christian love prompted him to do it. He secured a good guide, and found his way in time through the vast wilderness.

As for me, I little dreamed of anything unusual to happen on my return. As I approached our camp with my game on my shoulder, I had not the slightest premonition that I was suddenly to be hurled from my savage life into a life unknown to me hitherto.

When I appeared in sight my father, who had patiently listened to my uncle's long account of my early life and training, became very much excited. He was eager to embrace the child who, as he had just been informed, made it already the object of his life to avenge his father's blood. The loving father could not remain in the teepee and watch the boy coming, so he started to meet him. My uncle arose to go with his brother to insure his safety.

My face burned with the unusual excitement caused by the sight of a man wearing the Big Knives' clothing and coming toward me with my uncle.

"What does this mean, uncle?"

"My boy, this is your father, my brother, whom we mourned as dead. He has come for you."

My father added: "I am glad that my son is strong and brave. Your brothers have adopted the white man's way; I came for you to learn this new way, too; and I want you to grow up a good man."

He had brought me some civilized clothing, At first, I disliked very much to wear garments made by the people I had hated so bitterly. But the thought that, after all, they had not killed my father and brothers, reconciled me, and I put on the clothes.

After a few days, Ohiyesa started for the United States with his father. His heart was heavy.

For now all my old ideas were to give place to new ones, and my life was to be entirely different from that of the past.

Still, I was eager to see some of the wonderful inventions of the white people. When we reached Fort Totten, I gazed about me with lively interest and a quick imagination.

My father had forgotten to tell me that the fire-boat-walks-on-mountains had its track at Jamestown, and might appear at any moment. As I was watering the ponies, a peculiar shrilling noise pealed forth from just beyond the hills. The ponies threw back their heads and listened; then they ran snorting over the prairie. Meanwhile, I too had taken alarm. I leaped on the back of one of the ponies, and dashed off at full speed. It was a clear day; I could not imagine what had caused such an unearthly noise. It seemed as if the world were about to burst in two!

I got upon a hill as the train appeared. "O!" I said to myself, "that is the fire-boat-walks-on-mountains that I have heard about!" Then I drove back the ponies.

My father was accustomed every morning to read from his Bible, and sing a stanza of a hymn. I was about very early with my gun for several mornings; but at last he stopped me as I was preparing to go out, and bade me wait.

I listened with much astonishment. The hymn contained the word Jesus. I did not comprehend what this meant; and my father then told me that Jesus was the Son of God who came on earth to save sinners, and that it was because of him that he had sought me. This conversation made a deep impression upon my mind.

Late in the fall we reached the citizen settlement at Flandreau, South Dakota, where my father and some others dwelt among the whites. Here my wild life came to an end, and my school days began.